D1239231

To the Customers,
Clients and Friends
of Affiliated
Warehouse Companies.

— AlexSandra Lett

A Timeless Place

Lett's Set a Spell at the Country Store

AlexSandra "Sandy Lynn" Lett

A Timeless Place
Lett's Set a Spell at the Country Store

ISBN 0-9613649-1-2

Library of Congress Number 00-192865

476 / 3000

Limited edition hardback published by

TRANSFORMATIONS

1996 Buckhorn Road
Sanford, NC 27330-9782
USA
LettsSetaSpell@aol.com

Visit the world wide web:
http://www.atimelessplace.com

For more information contact:

AlexSandra "Sandy Lynn" Lett

at

(919) 777-9362

Dedicated

to my birth family

who brought me to earth

and

to my spiritual family

who keep me focused on heaven

*Are there precious people
who live in our hearts forever?*

*Are there keepsake places that dwell
tenderly in our minds?*

*Take a nostalgic journey to Buckhorn in rural
North Carolina...where colorful characters live
forever through spell-binding stories.
Join author AlexSandra Lett for a
heart-warming visit to a by-gone era
when her Grandpa's country store was
the social center of the community.
The store is closed now, with Grandpa
long gone, but the stories live on.
So pull up a chair, and
"set a spell."
Come on in to a timeless place
where love and laughter reign.
Lett's "set a spell" at the country store with
"Sandy Lynn" and the gentle souls who know
life is ripe for the pickin' every day.*

A Timeless Place

Lett's Set a Spell at the Country Store

Grandpa behind the counter at his country store

Chapter 1

Come on in, 'set a spell' at Grandpa's country store

Growing up on a huge farm in the middle of Nowhere — 12 long miles from a Somewhere called Sanford and four miles from a no-stoplight town known as Broadway — I figured out at an early age that Grandpa's country store was the social center of the Buckhorn community. On chilly days and nights local folks would hang out around Grandpa's old potbellied stove in the back room to catch up on the latest gossip.

On summer evenings farmers "set a spell" outside and compared tobacco prices and crop yields while wives shelled peas for tomorrow's supper.

There were off-color jokes, funny stories, character portrayals, and sometimes tragic news...all told with fervor and passion as folks "Lett" it all hang out. Some were recovering from 4 a.m. risings to take dried tobacco out of the barn, then prime more tobacco, loop it and put it into the barn for curing. Farmers, wives and "young'uns" came nightly to the community waterhole for "shooting the breeze" and thirst-quenching — only "dranks" mind you, ranging from Coca-Colas and Pepsis to Royal Crown colas, Spurs and chocolate-flavored sodas. Buying a nickle "drank" from the icebox was admission to the best show in the neighborhood — taking part in the real life daily drama series at the country store.

A few folks bragged about white lightning and homemade wine, but public partakings were few and far between. Sometimes I'd see Grandpa go quietlike behind the long counter — laced with hoop cheese, two-for-a-penny cookies and one-cent pieces of candy in big jars — and take a nip from an unlabeled bottle, but we'll talk about that later.

Upon entering the store customers were drawn
to mouth-watering favorites like vanilla cookies,
peppermint sticks, peanut brittle squares, and 3-D candy
(chocolate, vanilla and strawberry) but then there was
the gag-a-maggot item, pickled pig's feet. Ugh!
The shelves behind the counter featured boxes of candy
bars — on the bottom row so little hands could reach.
Other shelves held staples like pork 'n beans, vienna
sausages, sardines, and crackers. Heaven forbid anyone
who tried to eat sardines in the sanctuary of the store
'cause Grandpa would say "get those stinkin' 'thangs'
out of here."

Two cold bins, one for the many "drank" varieties,
the other for milk and ice cream, lined the right side.
The back area hosted a rack containing white loaf bread,
honey buns, oatmeal cream pies and moon pies, and of
course, nabs galore, those orange square crackers and
the round Ritz-like variety, both filled with peanut
butter, and a main staple in every farm worker's diet.

A main feature of the store was tobacco — rows of cigarette cartons, packages of chewing varieties, and cans of snuff. Sometimes the air would be thick with smoke from farmers who believed in supporting the tobacco industry. Anyone was welcome to contribute to the large can that once held peaches but now served as a spittoon. Ping! Ping! — the sound of gushing spit could not be mistaken. Chink! Chink! — one could hear as checkers were snapped on top of one another. The aroma of slightly burned coffee wafting through the air was all-too-familiar when the potbellied stove was fired up.

Anything could become a tall tale at Grandpa's country store in Buckhorn community where local yokels, "drank" salesmen and cracker carriers gathered daily to "set a spell." It didn't matter that bread and milk cost twice as much at Lett's Grocery as it did at the A & P uptown. This unofficial country club offered personal advantages that competitors couldn't match — here you could learn everything from who picked a mess of beans that day to who was messin' around with whom.

Nothing was too trivial to talk about...and no one was spared the threat of gossip. The key was to keep your nose clean and your drawers on — and, of course, go to church every Sunday — if you wanted to escape the wrath of wagging tongues. Anybody who broke the Ten Commandments could be "pert-near" burned at the stake on winter days by the potbellied stove in the back room. Many a stone was thrown at sinners on summer evenings a few yards from the store's shelter where people kept their distance from the bugs seeking the light.

This was before bug zappers, mind you. Oh, to be a fly on the wall or should I say, a bug near the bulb!

Lett's Grocery and Filling Station was situated in the Buckhorn vicinity in central North Carolina near the site where my ancestors originally settled. In 1739 a ship loaded with men, women and children from various countries came to this new land America via the Atlantic Ocean. The immigrants, including some Letts from Ireland, surveyed the Wilmington area and decided to head up the Cape Fear River in search of a prized possession: land they could claim. They stopped long enough to build flat-bottomed boats, rafts and dugouts to bring their belongings up the river.

The Lett family stayed a while at several places and in 1745 my ancestors rowed to the foot of Buckhorn Falls where they found what they were looking for: thousands of acres of rich bottom lands for growing cotton and other crops. The settlers marked their chosen site and called it Lett's Landing, which is still owned by family members today.

My great-grandfather John Wesley Lett, born in 1852, and my great-grandmother M. Arnettie Thomas, born in 1869, brought 10 new Letts into the world. Rumor has it that Grandpa — Willie Puzie Lett — was named after a preacher who conducted a revival at Moore Union Congregational Christian Church. It sounds like Pue-z, as in church pew — but sometimes misspelled Pusie and often mispronounced deliberately by "dirty minds."

This name, also passed onto my father, was a bone of contention throughout my childhood days as bad boys and sometimes prospective suitors teased me relentlessly.

Grandpa, born in 1888, inherited land near Lett's Landing and later bought a big house and farm for his wife and nine children three miles up the road. He was fondly called "Captain Puzie" and demanded respect and admiration with his captivating personality, tall stature, and big-brimmed hat. He was a handsome devil sporting a twinkle in his eye...with a yarn or joke for every man, a tease and treat for every child, and a smile and wink for all the women.

"Captain Puzie" was charming and comical...a butter-wouldn't-melt-in-his-mouth type of man, and a favorite with the ladies and the not-so-ladylike suitors who thought he had deep pockets. People were always trying to fix Grandpa up with a new Mrs. since "Miss Verta," my grandmother, died in 1952.

There was never a dull moment at Lett's Grocery and Filling Station and no end to folks trying to marry off Grandpa. One day John Henry Jackson, the Dr. Pepper salesman I dubbed "Mr. No Salt," brought the "dranks" to the store and was really excited because he had finally found Grandpa the perfect mate. This guy raved about a wonderful widowed woman and then pointed out that she too owned a country store.

He said to Grandpa, "You're going to love this woman because she's a lot like you. Her name is Mert Moore."

Without batting an eye Grandpa shot back, "Yes, I do love her...she's my sister."

Oh well...so much for match-making Grandpa.

The life and times at Lett's Grocery and Filling Station offered entertainment in the days before radio and television and continued to do so even after the talking box and "boob tube" started stealing people's brains..."tools of the devil," as Grandpa would say. The station WGCS (Grandpa's Country Store) signal came in loud and clear "pert-near" 16 hours every day from sunup to bedtime.

The colorful characters in the Buckhorn community were just as interesting as any movie star, soap opera idol or TV headliner. For example, before *I Love Lucy*, there was a neighbor named Penny Wellington, famous for her flaming red hair and weird sense of humor. She talked funny and acted crazy...some say she was not playing with a full deck.

One day Penny came into the store wearing miss-matched clothes as usual, carrying a six-pack of empty soda bottles, and babbling on and on about nothing that made any sense. Suddenly she yelled, "Captain Puzie, whatcha want me to do with these here 'drank' bottles?"

Grandpa said, "Just throw them over in the corner."

So she did.

It took a long time to pick up all that glass.

The country store is closed now, with Grandpa long gone, but the stories live on. So pull up a chair, and "set a spell"...

Cape Fear River

Chapter 2

Drawing upon the resources of the Cape Fear River

The Cape Fear River has always played an
important role in the life of the Letts and with lots
of other folks in the Buckhorn community.
Grandpa grew up at Daniels Creek near Lett's Landing,
and families who lived near the river depended on it
for part of their livelihood.

"We enjoyed fishing for fun but also for food," Grandpa would say. "We did a lot of work along the river, we even built a dam," he told me.

In 1900 the heirs of Andrew J. Lett sold about 10 acres next to a mill near Buckhorn Falls to Carolina Power and Light Company (CP&L) for $250, however a dam was never erected there. Meanwhile, the Cape Fear Power Company completed construction of a dam near the falls in about 1905, but never produced any electrical power. Since the river had not yet been tamed, floods did a lot of damage to the existing dirt dams. Eventually the company went into receivership and was sold at the courthouse in Chatham County. The new owners re-designed the project and resumed work on the dam.

Many of the men in Buckhorn community and surrounding areas helped build the dam and earned about 50 cents a day. Unfortunately, the loss of some lives was part of the price paid for electricity in the area. Grandpa said five men once lost control of their vessel and four of them went over the dam and drowned, including a foreman named Captain Thorson, whose fiance was en route to Raleigh from Minnesota.

"When she got here she had brought along a fancy frock for the wedding only to learn of her boyfriend's death," Grandpa said. "Her dreams died along with him," he added as his voice trailed off.

On September 3, 1907 while Grandpa was working on the dam a severe thunderstorm came up. He and about 50 construction workers took refuge in a cement house that was struck by lightning. Grandpa's brother Edd was hit, and the men put him under the drip of the house where the falling rain could revive him. "The lightning burned the strings right out of Edd's shoes," Grandpa said.

"It scared the living daylights out of me," he told me. Seven men, including two descendents of the Lett slaves, Talley and Rufus, were killed and another 20, counting Edd, injured by the lightning.

The project continued. W.M. Morgan, a Wake County man who founded CP&L, received a franchise from the City of Fayetteville to supply power for electricity. The first transmission line in the area, a 36-mile link supported by a single pole tower structure, was built from Buckhorn to Fayetteville. The first poles were placed on Lett property as the line continued its journey to Fayetteville.

The flip of a switch in Fayetteville on January 1, 1908 signaled completion of the project and creation of a large electrical supply to several areas. Eventually the Buckhorn plant near the dam became a prime source of power for Fayetteville, Jonesboro and Raleigh. Carolina Power and Light Company was chartered in 1908 and acquired the plant shortly after completion. Unfortunately, the folks in Buckhorn community didn't benefit from all the work until the Rural Electric Association (REA) utility company harnessed the electrical power more than 30 years later.

The families of my Grandpa and Grandma were involved with history in the making. The land adjacent to Buckhorn Dam was owned by Matilda Elbert Womack and Elais Calvin Cox, who had several children, including a son Doyle and a daughter Verta, who eventually married my Grandpa. Even today people take Doyle Cox Road in Lee County to get to the dam that extends to Corinth in Chatham County.

In 1944 Grandpa got the "living daylights" scared out of him again. "It was exciting but also scarey when all of a sudden we had bright lights everywhere," he said.

At last, electricity came to Buckhorn and brought light and delight to folks who "set a spell" at Grandpa's house and country store.

Meanwhile back at the river, folks in Buckhorn community and for many miles around relished its resources. While growing up, seining was a favorite sport for the Lett "young'uns" even though it was illegal to use this net method for catching fish.

Through the years the area near Lett's Landing became known as the ideal outlet to the Cape Fear River "where fish jump on the hook," according to Grandpa's nephew Wes, son of Edd and Ida Womack Lett. As a young man Wes' pet peeve was dealing with game wardens but most of the time he stayed two steps ahead of them. "They were always picking on me and had it in for me," he commented.

The game warden "pert-near" lived on the Lett property, determined to get those Lett boys, Wes said.

One day Wes was charged with fishing without a license. When he went to court he took all his brothers who looked like him, so when the game warden was asked to identify the guilty man, he couldn't. The case was dropped.

Another time Wes received a citation for fishing without a license and seining. If found guilty, he would have to pay a fine of $25, "which was a whole mess of money back then," he said. It took two days for the judge to find jury members who said they could be neutral about the case. Many folks said they couldn't judge Wes because he was such a good fellow and besides, he had let them go fishing on his property. Even when a jury was finally selected, they found him "not guilty."

His lawyer was Bill Staton, who went on to become a senator, and of course, enjoyed coming out to Lett's Landing on a regular basis for fishing and socializing.

Wes inherited prime property next to Lett's Landing and became known as the "gatekeeper" because he decided who passed through his property for fishing and hunting. He said "many a friend has been made" as folks stopped to ask for the privilege of entering the wilds of the woods and onto the grassy shores surrounding Cape Fear River. For the past half-century Wes has literally held the key to the most popular fishing hole in many counties. In recent years his cousin Gilbert opened up another road to the river and installed a large sign "Lett's Landing."

Through the centuries the river has offered hundreds of families the opportunity for food and fun as well as the gift of electrical power. As Grandpa once told me, "The Cape Fear River is 'pert-near' the best thing in Buckhorn."

Grandpa at the Stevens Cotton Gin in Broadway

Chapter 3

Survivors -- Making a living on the family farm

After Grandpa married Verta Cox, they inherited
56 acres at Daniels Creek on the Cape Fear River but
couldn't depend on the river for their livelihood.
Like many families they wanted to focus on farming,
however their land was thick with trees so not well suited
for cotton and other crops.

As the couple's "young'uns" came along they needed more open space for growing vegetables and fruits and increasing their crop yields. In 1925 the family of nine relocated about three miles west and began sharecropping with a man named John Harrington. They moved into a large two-story house featuring big porches upstairs and downstairs. At the time this seemed like a mansion.

"We felt like we had all died and gone to Heaven having all that space," Grandpa told me, "We even had plenty of room for two more 'young'uns' who came along later."

Eventually Grandpa and Grandma had nine children, starting with the birth of Gladys in 1908 and ending with Bettie in 1931. There were five other daughters, Esther, Alice, Cleo, Violet, and Selma, and two sons, Puzie (Bud) and Gilbert. Large families were necessary on the farm to handle the many chores and field work.

The Letts continued to use the land at the river for growing corn and pasturing cows during the summer.

Every spring Grandpa would tie the lead cow to the back of a wagon and the herd would follow her three miles down the road to spend the summer at the other farm. In the fall the cows were led back up the hill for grazing on the big farm.

Life on the farm consisted of long days — literally working from sunup to sundown. The Great Depression of 1929 and the following Recession spawned years of lack and deprivation, which increased and intensified the constant chores.

Grandpa summed up the cause of the Depression by saying "the rich got richer and the poor got poorer."

"City slickers were just plain greedy," Grandpa told me. "They wanted more than their share of everything...wanting to live high on the hog."

"When people get into the almighty dollar they forget the almighty God," he said. "They are doomed to fall flat on their faces."

Very little money was available for about 10 years, so almost everything was acquired through bartering and trading goods at stores. Families grew big gardens, harvested small grains crops such as corn, and had cows for milk and butter.

Doyett Lett works hard on the farm

Chickens were raised on the Lett farm for food and to provide a steady supply of eggs, which were used for bartering at a country store in Broadway, owned by Grandpa's sister Mert Moore and her husband Ernest. Traps were set for catching rabbits and squirrels, which could be traded at the farmers' market for mountain apples, bananas and other produce.

"Sometimes things got so tight with us we had to sell most of our eggs and country ham in order to get sugar, coffee, salt and pepper at Mert's store," Grandpa said.

During the many lean years the Lett family became even more entrepreneurial in order to survive. Grandpa had a cane mill where families traded 25 percent of their crop in order to get the cane made into syrup. One of the children fed the cane through a mule-drawn press while Grandpa used a wood-fired pan for cooking it into syrup. Since the family accepted syrup for payment and grew their own cane they had plenty to spare and share. Neighbors brought their own jugs and paid 25 cents a gallon for the syrup.

Grandpa also provided a saw-sharpening service for local saw mill operations. In the fall Grandpa and the "young'uns" cut and hauled a year's supply of stove wood for cooking and heating the house and also for firing the tobacco barns in the upcoming harvest season. During the cold months the family made handles for small tools from hickory logs and sold them for 25 cents each.

"We did everything we could just to survive," Grandpa said. "We had to eat and see that our neighbors did too."

In fact, these difficult times led some folks in many places to make moonshine and sell it just to be able to put food on the table and clothes on their children's backs, Grandpa told me. "They meant nobody any harm but some of them ended up in jail," he said.

For a long time cotton was the main income-producer on most farms in central North Carolina. Grandpa would leave home around 4 a.m. with a wagon full of cotton for the gin in Broadway while Grandma and the kids picked about 200 pounds each of the white fluffy stuff. It was a delight when any of the "young'uns" got to ride with Captain Puzie to the gin. Afterwards he'd take the lucky passengers by Moore's Country Store for treats, such as loose saltine crackers from a barrel and hoop cheese displayed on the counter. When Grandpa arrived home from the gin they loaded the cotton for the next day's trip. Infestation by the boll weevil changed all that, causing crop yields to plummet 50 percent.

In the 1930s tobacco began to sell at higher prices —
up to 30 cents a pound. As tobacco gained popularity
farmers became excited about its earning potential
and wanted to grow as much as possible. However,
government controls prevented that. Grandpa said
people got "mighty upset" about the small allotments
and began to rebel. In 1938 the controls were removed
and "all hell broke loose," according to Grandpa.

"We carried tobacco to the market and were offered
10 cents a pound, and we got so mad we brought it
back home," he told me.

Farmers welcomed the return of controls and by
1940 tobacco became the dominant crop in the
Buckhorn community.

For years Grandpa had to give the landlord 50 percent
of the money the family earned from cotton and
tobacco, and 25 percent from the grain crops,
such as corn, wheat and oats. The emergence of
tobacco as a money crop gave Grandpa enough cash
flow to buy a new truck in 1937 and to buy more land.
Eventually he accumulated 400 acres at this site,
and tobacco continued to be king for many years.

Despite the scarcity of many items during World War II, including clothes, shoes, coffee, candy, chewing gum, and gas, families coped on the farm. Trucks sat idle because gas couldn't be bought anywhere, but the old faithful horse and wagon got them through. Mules continued to be used to drive the sleds to the barn after tobacco was primed.

After surviving with lack during the Depression, Recession and the Big War, Grandpa vowed to never deal with shortages again. In 1946 he and a crew erected a two-room building for a country store and opened Lett's Grocery and Filling Station. Here he stocked all the staples such as bread, milk and hoop cheese plus a wide range of items suitable for "fast feeding" — ranging from "dranks" and chocolate sodas to nabs and moon pies. Also, he had plenty of gas for the family farm as well as for passersby.

The Lett farm and most others in Buckhorn community continued to prosper, and as Grandpa would say, "Finally, we were living the good life!"

Chapter 4

Love and war, then a new life...ripe for the pickin'

There was something special to remember for anyone who "set a spell" at Lett's Grocery and Filling Station in Buckhorn community. True stories, tall tales, juicy gossip and worn-out jokes at Grandpa's country store fostered never-to-be-forgotten recollections, and some favorites were passed along as a kind of natural oral history.

There was one story I never tired of hearing over and over again...how Dad married Mom before he went off to war. He was drafted into the U.S. Army during World War II, trained at nearby Ft. Bragg and then transferred to Camp Lee, Va. He came home on leave in the spring of 1942, and he and Mom decided to get married. She bought a purple and gold dress for the ceremony. Puzie Doyle Lett, better known as Bud, and Ruby Turner Knight rode down to Cheraw, S.C., and spoke their vows before a justice of the peace. They had only a few days together before Dad had to report to Ft. Dix, N.J.

Weeks later the summons came for Dad to go overseas to war, and he went away for two years and nine months. Mom would say woefully, "I forgot the sound of his voice." Sometimes the letters were delayed for weeks, but no news was good news. Dad came home only once from the war and then left again for another whole year. He served his country in Iceland and the European Theatre of Operations in the battles of Normandy, southern and northern France, and Rhineland.

Ruby Knight Lett and Puzie Doyle (Bud) Lett married on Friday, April 2, 1942. After being married four days, he left for duty with the U.S. Army and served in World War II.

During the war Mom stayed with her parents and family about eight miles away. She would send a post card to Grandpa when she wanted him to pick her up for a visit with the in-laws. As the wife of a soldier Mom got a $50 check each month from the U.S. Government and deposited every cent into a savings account, building a nest egg for herself and Dad. He sent her $15 a month for clothes, writing paper and postage.

Dad returned home with medals and battle scars — not from injuries but from a heavy heart, the kind that comes from too much killing and too little neighboring. He and Mom had written letters about having a baby, and nine months and four days after Dad wiped his hands of war, my brother, James Doyle (Jimmy) Lett, was born. No more Puzies, thank God. They stayed with Grandpa and Grandma for a while and then settled down in a farmhouse across the road from the homeplace and country store. Within a year my sister, Mary Carolyn, was born, named after my Mom's mother.

The love letters that had traveled from battle sites were tucked away in a dresser drawer, out of sight, out of mind but not hidden from the hearts of Mom and Dad. There were no vivid television scenes to replace war's flashbacks on my father's inner screen. The loneliness that had lurked in Mom's soul for four long years took a while to heal. Nevertheless, Dad had survived the war, and every day brought its own miracles.

With the love of his life by his side and a new daughter and growing son, Dad made a fresh start on the farm, rich with promise. He and Mom put their name on a waiting list for a "citified" automobile from the local dealership. They were disappointed when a couple down the road got the next one by mistake, but it turned out that car was a lemon. Soon afterwards, Mom and Dad paid $1,900 cash for a flashy blue and white 1949 Chevrolet that never gave them a minute's problem...and they kept it long after they bought their next car, a 1964 Chevrolet.

Bud and Ruby with Jimmy and Carolyn

Back then life was perfect...a couple passionately in love with each other, living in gratitude as war's horrors faded into the background, and raising their children in a farmhouse and owning a brand spanking new '49 Chevrolet. Like the strawberries in spring and the tobacco in summer, life was ripe for the pickin' and anything was possible...and everything was a blessing.

Little did they know as they settled into the peacefulness of normal everyday life their "oddball" child was on the way. And then came trouble!

Breech born with bronchitis...my difficult arrival into this world seemed symbolic of the chaos that seemed to follow me. In fact sometimes that chaos would wait in the wings until I caught up with it.

Mom and Dad named me Sandra Lynn, called me "Sandy" but hollered "Sandy Lynn" in a shrill voice when I didn't live up to their expectations of what a God-fearing Christian girl and well-mannered southern lady should be like. More often I did not.

As the 1949 car rusted out in the back yard, it became my first hideaway where I wrote articles for the school newspaper and poems just because. On winter days the car was warmer than the old farmhouse and away from the chitter-chatter and pitter-patter of too many folks yakking all the time.

I decided that making up my own stories was more interesting than participating in a farm family's drama because I could invent bold and beautiful people and create exciting experiences in faraway places.

Often I dreamed of meeting a prince who would rescue me from country folks and farm chores and who would let me sing, play the piano and write all day in his palace and, of course, live happily ever after.

I eventually learned that true love is not about knights in shining armor and there is a price to pay for being a writer, but that's another story for another day.

Mom's purple and gold wedding dress is tucked away in a cedar chest in their farmhouse, along with a heart-shaped gold locket featuring two small pictures of Bud and Ruby Lett taken before the war. Mom and Dad just celebrated their 58th wedding anniversary. Life on the farm is still ripe for the pickin' every day. Jimmy and Carolyn married well and have a whole bunch of "young'uns" and grandkids. I'm still waiting for the love of my life.

Chapter 5

Radio brings new worlds and soap operas to Buckhorn

In the good old days life on the farm was not all work and no play. While the juicy gossip and tall tales continued to highlight conversings at Grandpa's farmhouse and country store there was a whole new cast of characters inside the radio box that meddled more and more each moment in folks' everyday lives.

When oil lamps were used to eat by and read by and the evenings a little too quiet, the sound of other voices was a welcome reprive. The invention of the radio opened up new worlds to country folks back in the 1930s. The first radios originated before electricity so they ran on batteries, and sometimes listeners would cut the radio off during commercial breaks to make the batteries last longer.

Some radios were floor models, so large and well-made that they became prime pieces of furniture in a living room or parlor. The old-time antennas, often called aerials, were 100 feet long and strung up on a tree, and some were covered with a glass insulator to keep from shorting out. Radios depended on these aerials for picking up the programs so even the smaller table models couldn't be moved from room to room where chores could be handled nearby.

Grandpa was backward 'bout some things, and especially new gadgets, but he succumbed to the attraction of the new invention called the radio.

Grandpa bought one for the big farmhouse, and he and Grandma and nine children would gather around it on Saturday nights to hear the *Grand Ole Opry*. Grandpa told me they also loved to listen to Uncle Dave Macon, "who could play the bango 'pert-near' better than anyone." When neighbors stopped by to "set a spell" the house got crowded mighty fast.

Mom's family had a radio before she married Dad in 1942 and when Dad was serving in World War II, they followed news of defeats and victories. When he was gone for two years and nine months without coming home, Dad's voice drifted farther and farther away while new friends on the radio helped to soothe the pain. When letters were lost for weeks Mom turned to the radio for news that his location had not become a battle site, and that he was safe. When Mom's own soap opera was a little too painful to bear it was nice to meet other folks on radio's daytime dramas.

Yes, with the radio came the birth of soap operas. Mom told me that women would organize their days around their "stories" as they became an essential ritual of everyday life. Mom and other women liked to plan their ironing sessions and sewing tasks around such favorites as *The Guiding Light, Portia Faces Life, Backstage Wife, Road of Life, Lorenzo Jones,* and *Our Gal Sunday.*

As their own world spinned with seasons laden with happiness and tears, their stars laughed, cried, fell from grace and rose to greatness. Farm women and housewives all over the world fell prey to the lives of other men and women, often "citified" folks whose eloquent language mystified them almost as much as their powerful stories. Soap opera writers created serial dramas that revolved around the institution of the family and portrayed the life-giving strength that comes from a secure family unit and the destructiveness its members can unconsciously wreak on one another.

The Guiding Light, which began in 1937, was considered the most inspirational radio drama.

Its title stems from the first character the show introduced, the Rev. Dr. John Ruthledge, whose reading lamp in the window served as a guide for troubled parishioners. He was minister of the Little Church of Five Points, located in a suburb of Chicago. Before the Reverend died he passed the light on. Eventually the locale of this longest running soap opera was changed to Springfield, a town somewhere in the Midwest.

For many years the plot focused on the trials of the wise immigrant Papa Bauer (played by Theo Goetz) and his daughter-in-law Bert (played by the Charita Bauer for three decades). Bert's son, Dr. Ed Bauer, brought his patients into women's living rooms all over the world, and when they died, women and children mourned as if they were kinfolk.

One day Dad was supposed to help his brother Gilbert at his cabinet shop but told him he couldn't come because of a funeral. When Gilbert wanted to know who had died Dad mentioned someone on *The Guiding Light*, and they roared with laughter.

As for an update on the other soaps, that's another story for another day!!!

By the late 1930s, more than 30 radio serials reached a daily audience of 40 million. This huge audience was a bonanza for program sponsors. Ma Perkins, a successful radio serial, sent the sales of Oxydol, a laundry detergent, through the roof.

Soap companies plunged into the business of producing serials that featured their products, and they so dominated daytime that serials became known as soap operas. Their popularity led Proctor & Gamble to sponsor numerous additional soap operas. Meanwhile loyal listeners became faithful buyers of P&G brands.

Mom admitted that while shopping in the big grocery stores she bought the detergents advertised on her favorite daytime dramas. These cleansers also contained different types of dishes so homemakers relished opening laundry detergent boxes to view their latest prized possessions...a cup trimmed in pale pink roses or a fancy glass featuring fruit designs. Food boxes carried surprises too, such as glasses in a box of oats...sometimes called the poor girl's crystal.

Even some of the peanut butter brands and jellies were packed in beautiful glasses that featured modern-day heros from radio and TV programs.

The soap operas were meant to be about ordinary lives of ordinary people in ordinary towns of the time, although it was extraordinary how many affairs, divorces, surprise appearances and disappearances, exotic diseases, rare afflictions like amnesia, murders, and kidnappings befell such a few people in such small towns. Whatever problems and pitfalls characters encountered in their pursuit of the American Dream, listeners never ceased to believe in it. The tragedies on soap operas were mostly due to natural disasters or human failings rather than divine intervention, but this factor didn't seem to conflict with country folks' steadfast belief in predestination, God, marriage, motherhood, apple pie or the old-fashioned morals. Besides, the soaps gave country folks a whole new cast of characters to include in their updates of the latest gossip while "shooting the breeze" at the farmhouse and the country store.

Puzie Lett, fondly called "Captain Puzie"

Chapter 6

Air-wave friends and enemies visit country folks

Come on in... "set a spell" by the potbellied stove
in the back room of Grandpa's country store.
The women folk must let the big boys do what they do
best — make macho, even though that word would
have never been used in the 1930s when boxing made
its debut on the newest form of entertainment: radio.

Imagine it's June 22, 1938, and the biggest night in the history of sports so far. This is the match when Joe Louis, the Brown Bomber of Detroit and the Heavyweight Champion of the World, knocks out Max Schmeling in a return bout to avenge an earlier defeat. From 1934 on Louis had won over greats like Primo Carnera, Kingfish Levinsky, Max Baer, and Paolino Uzcudum but got cocky and lost to German fighter Schmeling in the summer of 1936.

During the rematch between Louis and Schmeling the country was caught up in the symbolism of a black man fighting a representative of Nazi Germany's master race. Everyone was backing Louis, who embodied the American ideal of a poor boy who made good. Louis was hailed as an American hero, especially after he donated some of his winnings to the Navy and Army relief funds. To further demonstrate his patriotism he enlisted in the Army in 1942, sacrificing his boxing career, and earning $21 a month instead of his usual $300,000 a year from boxing.

During the boxing matches, the other radio at
Grandpa and Grandma's house was quiet. Instead the
ladies and children were setting in the living room
eating popcorn and sharing juicy gossip...and of course,
discussing the latest goings and comings on the daily
soap operas.

A new way of life opened with radio — far
beyond the confines of country traditions, community
happenings, and church rituals. Horizons broadened
as they heard of faraway places and different types of
people. The thoughts held most sacred, the secrets
whispered under sheets at night, the things one did not
talk about in public suddenly blared along air waves
to disturb and yet to entertain the enchanted.

Radio dramas and traumas were shocking to the
simple folks in Buckhorn community and to other
vicinities formerly isolated from the cultural
complexities and vivid realities of the World Out There.
Country folks were frightened by change but equally
enamored by this whole new universe. Air-wave friends
and enemies came to reside in their minds and
sometimes their hearts.

Men and women folk and "young'uns" all got hooked on such shows as *Lum and Abner*. While priming tobacco they'd laugh about Lum and Abner, the main characters in a night-time drama about the everyday happenings in the sleepy little town of Pineridge in Arkansas. After the oil boom in Pineridge Lum and Abner started a matrimonial mail service to fix Abner up with the right woman, which led to many crazy adventures.

Meanwhile, long before Nathan Crissman married my cousin Mary Alice Lett, he fell prey to his favorite radio show, *The Hermit*, the one he loved and hated the most. His Mom and Dad would take all eight children across a valley on Sunday evenings where his Grandma and Grandpa — Ada Gwen and Nathan Dean Bryant — had the radio on. Other relatives would come to the homeplace in the Pocket community of Lee County, and the whole living room would be packed with people listening.

In *The Hermit* the narrator would say: "Turn your lights down low, this is the Hermit speaking." Nathan's Grandpa Bryant would lower the flame in the oil lamp and hush the children as the Hermit told scary stories. "We had to set there real quiet like," Nathan said. All would sit spellbound for a while and then one of the kids would always sneak around and touch someone's ear, and he'd squeal so loud the darkness would seem to break in two.

Going back home required walking across the dark valley again and the kids expected one of the wild creatures from *The Hermit* to jump into their path any minute.

Nathan's hero, Like most young boys', was the do-gooder masked man in *The Lone Ranger* (portrayed by Brace Beemer). Nathan said *The Lone Ranger*'s main advertiser was Merita bread and the masked man's picture was featured on the loaf. He and other boys saved bread wrappers to send in for Lone Ranger mementos.

Another sponsor of *The Lone Ranger*, the longest running children's show on radio from 1933 to 1956, was General Mills (Cheerios, Wheaties and Kix cereals), which offered various prizes and premiums for fans of the Lone Ranger and Tonto.

In one episode Sam Colt sent the Lone Ranger a ring with a miniature six-gun on top with symbols around it. The symbols included a bullet, representing the Lone Ranger's silver bullets, an Indian Arrowhead for Tonto's people, a Lone Star for Texas, and a horseshoe for luck or for his horse Silver. This story line led to the offering of the Lone Ranger Six-Gun Ring, available by sending in cereal box lids. Cousin Nathan proudly showed off his six-gun ring and talked endlessly about it to anyone who would listen.

During the 1948 season, many of the Lone Ranger's adventures took place in and around a western town called Frontier Town. One of the show's premiums was the Frontier Town, which came in four sections including cardboard buildings, bridges, Indian tepees and even the Lone Ranger's secret hideout. An enclosed map showed the layout of the town and its buildings, such as the Wells Fargo Express Office and the Powderhorn County Jail, as well as landmarks surrounding the town such as the Enchanted Hills and Sagebrush Hollow. Buildings were added by cutting them from specially marked boxes of Cherrios. The four sections of the map were obtained through the mail for a Cherrios box top and 10 cents for each section. There were a total of nine different Cherrios packages containing the buildings. When kids received the maps, additional buildings made of stiff paper were included, so they had to have the whole bundle for a complete town.

Nathan said the neat thing about this premium was that since most of the Lone Ranger's adventures in 1948 took place in and around the town, fans could follow the story step-by-step by laying out the map with all its buildings before each show. Many "younguns" did this over and over even though the fragile nature of the maps and cardboard buildings soon made it a frustrating chore. Nevertheless, Nathan said it was the king of all radio premiums for many kids.

Cousin Nathan said jokes sprung up about the favorite action hero. For example...

"Meanwhile back at the ranch...Tonto unaware that the Lone Ranger had disguised himself as a door up and shot his knocker off."

Role models like the masked man inspired Nathan to grow up and become the tax collector of Lee County, which instilled the wrath of God in local yokels who gave him hell when their taxes went up.

Meanwhile back at the country store...radio shows offered a whole new way of life for folks in Buckhorn but nothing could take the place of sharing neighbor-to-neighbor news and communing day in and day out with each other.

Grandpa "sets a spell" under the country store's shelter

*Grandpa's house was a popular place for family and friends
to watch the latest invention, "the television set"*

Chapter 7

The 'boob tube' begins reign and steals the brain

Picture this...a large square box brought into the living room of a farmhouse and becoming the focal point of family gatherings and community life.

Picture this...a 17-inch screen with scenes in black and white, or more like various shades of gray, featuring little talking people in distant places.

Enter the television set, and a big shock to country folks who had rarely traveled more than 50 miles from their place of birth.

It was one thing to experience the life and times of other cultures through listening to radio everyday or going to the talking motion picture once in a blue moon but to have a screen sitting in the living room spouting stories stranger than science fiction was the ultimate attraction and distraction.

As usual, Grandpa, who had deep pockets though he would never admit it, scowled over the prospect of spending money on another gadget, the television set. A TV was a prized piece of furniture — it cost about $200. Aunt Gladys, who lived with Grandpa, took the plunge and went up to the only appliance place within 15 miles and ordered one. When the television arrived in 1953 it was the first in the Buckhorn community.

At night after supper we left home and hearth
to explore adventures beyond our farmhouse.
As we walked across the road to Grandpa's house,
we crossed the door into a world like another planet.

I can remember the first program I ever watched,
I Love Lucy when I was about three years old.
I crawled into the big lap of my Aunt Gladys and
snuggled close to her big bosom (Lett women are
famous for their big boobs, so later I wondered if that
was the reason we came to call the TV the "boob tube.")
I stared at the television set, mesmerized by the antics
of Lucy and Ricky and others who loomed large and
mysterious in my mind. Like a fly on the wall I became
privy to "goings on" in another family's life right in
the middle of Grandpa and Gladys' living room.
Laughing with Lucy, laughing at Lucy, incapable of
moving, trancelike, I "set" right there and peed in my
pants! Aunt Gladys' loud yelp woke me from my spell,
as she ran for a towel to dry her frock.

That story of "Sandy Lynn" peeing in her pants in Gladys' lap became the latest scene in the ongoing soap opera in the community. From then on nobody could talk about *I Love Lucy* without mentioning me, and to this day no one has ever let me forget the incident.

Let me tell you about my cousin Eula's husband Gordon Wilson, who was a handy-man and while working at a large manufacturing company discovered he had a knack for fixing machines. When Eula and Gordon got their first TV and it broke, he figured out how to fix it himself. From there a new trade was born, and Gordon became king of TV repair in Buckhorn community and the greater Sanford area. He even opened his own store and repair shop.

In 1955 Daddy gave Mama a curing of tobacco to sell so she could buy something special -- a TV. I brought any chore I could to the living room, shelling peas from the couch, ironing while watching the soap operas, pretending I was Loretta Young on *The Loretta Young Theatre*, and imagining that I was a lucky little girl who was given a million dollars by Michael Anthony from *The Millionaire*.

I grew up with the Mousketeers, saw their first appearance on a special program celebrating the opening of Disneyland, and relished *The Mickey Mouse Club*. I idolized Annette Funicello, wanted desperately to be her, longed to own the official Annette Funicello watch (Mom and Dad bought me Cinderella instead), and eventually went to see all her movies.

I watched in awe *Father Knows Best* and *Leave It to Beaver* and believed that everyone else beyond Buckhorn community lived in nicer houses and that their Dads always wore Sunday go-to-meeting suits and their Moms kept house in church clothes and high heels. "Lettsville" grew smaller and less appealing each day as I got to know Jim and Margaret Anderson of Springfield and June and Ward Cleaver of Mayfield and the rebellious "Beaver" (not unlike the wild child "Sandy Lynn"). These people resided on a street surrounded by other houses. What...not everyone lived in a farmhouse in the middle of a field surrounded by 400 acres?

Now, I was never a carefree sort of kid...I thought too much, over-reacted to everything, and was over-sensitive. Television rattled my brain in a whole new way. Sorry, but I wasn't cut out to be a farm girl.... I was born to be a star, and I longed to dance, act, sing and play the piano, and travel far and wide. Back then Buckhorn community felt more like a jail cell in *Gunsmoke* than a scene in *The Waltons*. My family seemed more like *The Beverly Hillbillies* — we even had a Granny since Mom's mother Mary Knight looked enough like Granny Clampett to be her twin!

Grandpa loved to rant and rave about television. He'd say that family used to be with family, but now they cared more about the characters in the shows than they did their own kinfolks. They'd let a storm pass right by and leave their clothes on the line in pouring rain if someone was dying on *As The World Turns*.

Before someone coined the word "boob tube," Grandpa believed that if folks set in front of the TV they would go blind or become a boob, or a blooming idiot.

In his last days, Grandpa talked a lot about how he wished he never let that television set into his house because it was "the tool of the devil." It kept mamas from taking care of their "young'uns." It kept papas from tending their crops. It took folks away from church meetings and even interfered with visiting sick folks.

Grandpa was dead wrong about some things and rarely right about most issues 'cause he looked at things "pert-much" through the distorted mirrors of his own short-sighted eyes. But Grandpa was right about television — it can be evil if it takes country folks or even the most "citified" away from the things that matter most — home and family.

For a long time TV and other factors I deemed more important distracted me from appreciating the gifts offered by my family, by my community, and helped create my own tunnel-visioned drama. While my family will never be perfect like the Waltons, the Letts of Buckhorn community are "mighty fine" folks just the same.

Goodnight, Mary Ellen. Good night, John Boy. Good night, Gladys. Good night, Grandpa.

Dad shows off a prize catch

Chapter 8

Fishing, picking blackberries, fighting mosquitos and chiggers

Every family like every vicinity has its own way of celebrating holidays. While growing up in Buckhorn community in the 1950s and 1960s there "weren't" any discharging of cannons, ringing of bells, or drinking of toasts (perhaps some nipping behind closed doors) on Fourth of July.

Our parade consisted of Grandpa, Gladys, Mom, Dad and we three "young'uns" walking a bee line to a popular fishing hole about a mile from Grandpa's country store. There weren't any fireworks unless it was Grandpa or Dad raising Cain about us acting like wild alley cats. Now, country folks weren't much for what the "givernment" called holidays, 'cause Grandpa said such events were for "citified" people who had easy jobs with too much time on their hands. But on Independence Day my family usually avoided putting tobacco in the barn, and would cut back on farm chores so we could do something special.

One of my favorite Fourth of July outings was a trip to the river to fish — especially since we could pick and eat blackberries all along the way. Mom insisted we wear long-sleeved shirts and britches to avoid the attack of mosquitos and chiggers (also called redbugs) and to protect us from briars and brush on the long walk. With our handmade cane fishing poles and tin buckets in hand we headed off through the woods, blazing new trails and beating the bushes for fresh blackberries. Yum!

When we arrived at the so-called Kelly fishing hole we sat on the banks and ate blackberries while casting our poles into the water. What I hated most was baiting the hooks with live crickets and worms with the same fingers used for eating blackberries. I didn't mind the stained hands from natural blackberry dye but I felt guilty about killing those cute little worms and chirping crickets. When I asked my Dad, real nicelike, to "please, pretty please" bait the hooks he would usually do so without much hassle but my brother Jimmy would taunt me — "Are your hands broke?" or "Prissy little girl, can't even bait a hook!"

My big brother was a mean little rascal whose main purpose for living was making my life miserable. He lived to hassle me — whether it was teasing me about marrying some ugly boy in the neighborhood, kicking my cat George, or squeezing my boney arms until they were decorated with bruises.

Dad, Jimmy, my sister Carolyn, and I ate almost as many blackberries as we picked, despite Mom's protests, pigging out non-stop until we were bloated. Just as well our stomachs were full because by the time we got home we could hold back a little bit while Mom prepared a batch for a cobbler. Once back at the farm the menfolks would clean the fish (thank God), and we prissy girls would wash and cap the blackberries for dessert as well as get them ready for Mom and Gladys to preserve a dozen jars of blackberry jelly.

All of us practically dried up the well while hosing down our bodies in hopes of destroying Poison Ivy and Poison Oak just waiting to make our lives unbearable with itchy rashes.

We'd sit down to a "mighty fine" supper — fried fish, fried cornbread, homemade slaw, and of course, blackberry cobbler. Dad would get out the old ice cream freezer and get it cranking while we took turns churning the milk and sugar and vanilla flavoring into homemade ice cream.

Meanwhile Carolyn and I painted our chigger bites all over with fingernail polish, hoping to suffocate the redbugs that were eating us for supper. Come to think of it, the redbugs that burrowed in our skin were probably better for us than the dyes and chemicals in the polish, but it sure was fun polka dotting our whole body with the likes of Pink Passion and Red Rage!

The next morning Mom made pancakes, and while some folks preferred Karo syrup (the one that said on the label "gives your pancake a college education"), our favorite topping was blackberry jelly. You have not really tasted mouth-watering pancakes until you have eaten them with fresh blackberry jelly, a house speciality of "Ruby's Restaurant."

As we "younguns" turned into teenagers Mom and Dad would drive us to Sanford 12 miles away on Fourth of July so we could see the sky light up with fireworks. We watched in awe as someone somewhere stirred up a bunch of colorful explosions in the pitch black sky to lighten our spirits and brighten our lives.

One time Jimmy and some local yokels rode over to Conway, S.C. to buy the high-powered fireworks — the kind that could blow your arm off — and he and the Howard cousins and the Kelly brothers had their own hellfire and brimstone party. Oh, I forgot, I "won't" supposed to "tattle-tale" lest my brother tell Mama and Daddy that once I sat around smoking cigarettes with Patricia, Wanda and Barbara until I "pert-near" coughed myself to death.

Looking back I realize our celebration of Fourth of July reflected a greater reality — the American dream — and we experienced our freedom by roaming the woods, fetching a mess of food, and running wild. Yes, on the Lett farm in Buckhorn community life was ripe for the pickin' every day, even though at the time we didn't know we had it so good. We lived in a land of plenty — lots of fine folks, an abundance of good eating, and plenty of mosquite bites. Looking back we had "pert-near" anything country folk could ever "want for"!

Now, every Independence Day Grandpa is shining
down from the heavens and Gladys is kicking up
her heels 'cause she ain't canning and freezing.
We still miss them, especially on holidays, when
we're cooking and eating and talking a mile a minute
at my parents' farmhouse where life is ripe for the
pickin' every day...with or without blackberries!

Mom taking time out to play with "young'uns"

"Sandy Lynn" hanging out with Grandpa in 1970

Chapter 9

Feeling free — Born on the Fourth of July

While hanging out with Grandpa at the country store I learned a lot about life. For one thing Grandpa had his moments of genius. Now, most of the time he was a stubborn know-it-all but once in a blue moon he waxed poetic. Sometimes he'd rare back like a horse in heat and say excitedly, "Now listen to this, Sandy Lynn, you mark my word, there's a price to be paid for anything worth having."

While Grandpa loved being captain of his own ship —
the sole proprietor of Grandpa's country store —
owning a business wasn't just about listening to people
"shoot the breeze." Providing the place for community
gatherings carried with it responsibility — responding
to the needs of farmers and neighbors and passersby
by offering the finer things in life. While folks partook
of the "dranks," nabs, hoop cheese and cookies,
and of course, the basics like bread, milk, cigarettes
and gas, it "weren't" the refreshments and supplies
that local yokels enjoyed so much — but the supply
of country folks who gathered there and the
abundance of socializing and gossiping available.
Grandpa held down the fort "pert-near" 16 hours a
day for this center of community and communion.

One thing Grandpa loved was trivia and long
before the game "Trivial Pursuit" became popular
Grandpa was quizzing me and everyone about this
and that. For every customer he had a joke that they
were required to laugh at whether or not it was funny,

and some advice for everyone whether they wanted to hear it or not. Often he had pearls of wisdom to share, though sometimes it was hard to find them among all the gabbing.

Grandpa especially loved anything related to patriotic holidays and would get excited talking about the men, including his son and my father who fought in World War II. He would also tell me about stories related to the Revolutionary War and the Civil War. He could barely pronounce Declaration of Independence but he knew what it was, and he never took it for granted.

He especially liked a faded document, called Facts about the Declaration of Independence, written by "author unknown," which he hung on the counter in the country store.

The tattered piece of paper told about the ill fates of many of the men who signed the document on July 4, 1776 — outlining stories and sacrifices of the American Revolution.

The paper stated:

"These were not wild-eyed, rabble-rousing ruffians. They were soft-spoken men of means and education. They had security, but they valued liberty more. Standing tall, straight, and unwavering, they pledged: 'For the support of this declaration, with firm reliance on the protection of divine providence, we mutually pledge to each other, our lives, our fortunes, and our sacred honor.'

"They gave you and me a free and independent America. The history books never told you a lot about what happened in the Revolutionary War. We didn't fight just the British. We were British subjects at that time and we fought our own government! Some of us take these liberties so much for granted, but we shouldn't.

"Remember: freedom is never free!"

Meanwhile Grandpa also talked to me one day about other trivia related to the Fourth of July and Presidents of the United States. He said that exactly 50 years after the Declaration of Independence was signed Thomas Jefferson, the third president, died about noon at Monticello on July 4, 1826. Grandpa pointed out the irony of Jefferson, the author of the document, dying on its 50th anniversary.

What was even more "quar" (means queer or strange), according to Grandpa, is that John Adams, the second president, died on the same day as Jefferson six hours later at Quincy, Mass. Meanwhile Adams' son, John Quincy Adams, became the sixth president, making them the only father-son presidents to date.

Rumor has it that the fifth president, James Monroe, died on July 4, 1831, in New York City, where he had moved after financial problems forced him to sell his Virginia home.

While Grandpa and I liked to talk trivia and could spend hours yakking about nothing anyone else could find remotely interesting we had an understanding: he did most of the talking. When the air seemed thick with silence he felt obligated to fill it with "chitter chatter," but it was in the spaces between that we bonded most. He'd look at me with that twinkle in his eye and smile, and I'd grin from ear to ear. We didn't always agree on important things like religion and education but we were kindred spirits. We loved history and history in the making — we relished the ongoing story of various "hises" and "herses" who stopped to "set a spell" at Grandpa's country store.

Like Grandpa I grew up to be an entrepreneur, using my education and experience to write for readers and speak to audiences.

Like Grandpa I value the flexibility and freedom of my work, pumping out stories instead of gas, serving up food for thought instead of "dranks" and nabs, and remembering to often "set a spell" with the country folks who still have much to offer.

Like Grandpa I know the most important thing in life is feeling free, and we found it by living in a land of opportunity where we could turn our work into play. Even the times when we would work our fingers to the bone we could look forward to the times when we could talk trivia and do "pert-near" anything else we pleased.

Sure, sometimes freedom means honoring the "musts" and "shoulds" that dominate our society. More often freedom calls for standing up for our beliefs and standing for the people we love. The Declaration of Independence was signed by people who risked their lives so Grandpa and I could be free...and so each of us could live like we were born on the Fourth of July! Because we were!!!

Grandpa socializes at church

Grandma hosts a family gathering

Chapter 10

Grandpa's sermon:
'Give me that old-time religion'

On Sunday mornings my Grandpa used to drive
his truck slowly down the road picking up country
folks along the roadside for a ride to church.
The picker-uppers went to the Letts' home church,
Moore Union Congregational Christian Church,
located in Buckhorn community about four miles from
the country store.

Grandpa was a God-fearing man who took his religion seriously — and he had great expectations for the Sunday-go-to-meeting folks and especially the preacher. Not that Grandpa's nose was always clean, mind you, but that's another story for another day.

Rumor has it that one time a new preacher was voted on by the congregation and hired by the board of deacons. If I recollect correctly it had something to do with needing someone fast and making do with a young fellow fresh out of college who would accept the low pay offered by a small country church.

Back then it was customary for the preacher to ask someone else to do the closing prayer and then he'd go to the vestibule. This was the time when church members could shake the preacher's hand, brag about the sermon, or say something personal to the pastor at the door as they were leaving.

On the first Sunday after hearing a lengthy sermon my Grandpa looked the new minister straight in the eye and said, "You're something else."

The still-wet-behind-the-ears pastor was surprised about this comment and was even more curious the next Sunday when Grandpa shook his hand and said even more dramatically, "You're something else."

Now the minister got to thinking the next week that Grandpa must be bragging about him and that "something else" must mean that he was something special and doing a good job.

So the next Sunday when Grandpa repeated the ritual by saying "You're something else," the pastor responded. "Mr. Puzie, what do you mean by that?"

Grandpa shot back, "Well, you must be something else 'cause you sure ain't no preacher."

Needless to say that pastor didn't last long at Moore Union Congregational Christian Church because if Grandpa didn't like him and told everybody who "set a spell" at his country store, the preacher was doomed. Besides, half the congregation was related to Grandpa and the graveyard full of Lett tombstones. Between the live yakkers and the prevailing ghosts a lot of taunting and haunting took place.

Back then preachers were called to preach, or they weren't really preachers but disciples of the Devil, according to Grandpa. And when Grandpa believed in something he hammered it into your head until you finally said you agreed with him just to get him to quit badgering you.

I can remember hearing Grandpa preach many a sermon about just that...how the downfall of the old-time religion was coming about because the people in the pulpit weren't preachers at all but college-educated idiots. He said these new so-called ministers used "purty" words to describe God and fancy phrases about religion and could quote from the Good Book but something was missing. Like the cook who left the yeast out of the bread, these highly schooled pastors lacked the main ingredient for making people's religious life rise to ecstasy.

What was missing? Fire in the soul, according to Grandpa, and if they didn't have that they were doomed to hellfire and brimstone. The gift of gab wasn't enough — the voice of God raging through was the real power, not silvery tongues. Rantings and ravings about sin were natural for the true preachers who were expected to save souls and bring sinners to their knees. According to Grandpa, preachers who couldn't preach were rotten to the core. Every Sunday was a revival or it "weren't" no Sabbath at all!

Even on his death-bed Grandpa was still preaching the same old sermon, "Give me that old-time religion." I came from the Midwest to visit and sat by his bed as he told me over and over again about the decay of religion. I longed to hear it from the vibrant Captain Puzie who dramatically expressed his views with such self-appointed authority and self-righteousness.

On our final encounter I wished I had captured this colorful character on a home movie long ago while he was standing in his own pulpit at the country store speaking fervently about the old-time religion.
It was even too late to use my tape recorder because sentences were left hanging in mid-air as his voice trailed off to other subjects. By now I could fill in the gaps in his one-sided conversation.

I had long tired of this sermon, could quote it word for word, but I will never tire of hearing Grandpa tell his same old stories again and again.

But, Grandpa, if you were here today I would have just one thing to say, "You must be something else 'cause you sure ain't no preacher."

Chapter 11

Looking for Heaven beyond Grandpa's country store

There's a saying in the South that we gotta "run everything in the ground"...meaning we carry things too far. This shows up as telling people more than they want to know, wearing out our welcome, being nicey-nice when we can't stand the person we're talking to, and drinking oneself under the table.

Today's psychologists — "quacks," as Grandpa would say — might label it addictive behavior but Grandpa "purty much" called anything he didn't understand "poppy cock."

Now, when it came to most things, Grandpa would run them in the ground. He just couldn't stop himself. The truth is sometimes Grandpa was "bad to drink," which was the Southern way of saying he had too much moonshine or had fallen into a barrel of white lightning. The bottom line is that Grandpa couldn't hold his liquor.

When he was sober he could charm a snake out of a tree, and when he was nippy, he was the snake, so watch out! But whether Grandpa was two sheets to the wind or dry as a bone he was an expert on everything...sin, politics, tobacco, raising "young'uns," you-name-it. Whether preachin' from his self-erected pulpit next to the potbellied stove at his country store, or shouting his words at the counter laced with cookies and hoop cheese, he knew all about the old-time religion, and dammit, he was right.

Well, sometimes people teach what they most need to learn. Grandpa meant well, but after all, it was he who told me the road to hell was paved with good intentions. Impressive deeds alone didn't account for much either...it was kinda like putting fresh butter on stale bread or a brand spanking new Sunday suit on a spoiled soul.

Life was black and white for Grandpa — preachers who couldn't preach were rotten to the core...folks who didn't believe every word of the *Bible* were going straight to hell. When it came to his own transgressions, Grandpa found a gray area. And when it boiled down to his "drinking problem" the Devil had him by the balls.

Grandpa was heavily influenced by his best buddy, who I'll call Otis Campbell, his evil twin. With Otis Grandpa had his row to hoe. Otis practically lived at the country store, and was also planted in a bottle, the liquor bottle, that is. Together they were more likely to become "sots" than saints.

Behind closed doors — certainly not at the country store — everyone talked about Grandpa and his "burden" — in fact, folks say it was drinking that got him into big trouble one time. When no one knew I was listening I heard about Grandpa being involved with a wild woman. After his beloved wife died many women folk took a fancy to him and some to his deep pockets, but he never found another true love to have and to behold.

Folks say Grandpa would have never looked twice at that tramp he had taken up with if it hadn't been for the evil influence of too much booze. Finally Grandpa came to his senses about the wayward woman, repented and reclaimed his power as the preacher at his country store.

Growing up I was mighty confused. Grandpa and my parents told me that if I lived a good Christian life but went out with friends and drank one beer and then got killed in a car wreck I would go to Hell. Alcohol was the drink of the Devil, and if I ever let it touch my lips and go down my throat and drip on down to my stomach, I was a goner — unless I repented, of course. Yet Grandpa kept a bottle hidden under the counter and would take a nip now and then, and when he was high we knew he had nipped too much.

Grandpa and the whole family were fundamentalist Christians. They supposedly adhered to the Ten Commandments in the spirit and letter of the law, and anyone who broke them was doomed to spend eternity in Hell unless, of course, they repented.

When I talked to Grandpa, and Mom and Dad of my confusion about the horrors of Hell and how it made no sense to me, I was told "What would THEY say about your words?" THEY meaning people at the Letts' home church in Buckhorn community where we were spoon-fed rigid rules and dogmas every Sunday morning. As a little girl their beliefs made me cringe with fear and their views of sin and hellfire and damnation made me tremble in my tiny shoes.

When I asked them about the people in other countries who didn't even know about God, THEY said "we send missionaries there to minister to them." These foreign preachers and teachers traveled far to tell people about Jesus, the son of God, and how He could wash away our sins and save our souls from the raging fire. "Only through Jesus can people be saved," THEY would say.

What about the little girls and boys who never heard about Jesus? Sorry, THEY would say, they go straight to Hell.

What about the folks who did wonderful deeds and were really good people but hadn't been saved by Christ's blood? Sorry, THEY would say, they go straight to Hell.

Why, I wondered, is God creating all these human beings if most were doomed to spend eternity in Hell instead of enjoying everlasting life in Heaven?

Surely the God I envisioned was not the demanding, merciless Holy Man my family worshiped.

Even as a child I was fascinated by different ideas and sometimes spent my allowance on horoscope magazines that said the position of the planets affect us. I relished reading Eastern philosophy books that stated we were born into the body over and over again until we learned the lessons of unconditional love. My ancestors would roll over in their graves if they knew I was questioning anything THEY said.

The free spirit in me couldn't live in fear all the time... fear of not ever being good enough, fear of not being forgiven, fear of burning in Hell. Somehow there had to be a little bit of Heaven right here, right now, and I was determined to find it.

So I traveled far and wide — becoming "educated beyond my intelligence," according to my family — explored complex religions, highfalutin philosophies and complicated psychological ideas. But I never found the simple complacency I saw in the faces of the people who "set a spell" at Grandpa's country store.

They had found contentment with their teachin's and preachin's, and I eventually made peace with my beliefs about spirituality. If their religion made them happy, then it was good enough for me.

Sometime before Grandpa and Otis headed for the Big Blue Yonder they put down the bottle and never drank the Devil's Delight again. I bet Grandpa and Otis are up in Heaven getting in the last word about religion, shoving angels aside and putting educated preachers in their place. After all, Grandpa was called to preach and his sidekick Otis will always be in his Amen corner. I just know Grandpa is looking down from Heaven every day, saying to THEY and me, "Give me that old-time religion."

Chapter 12

White people vs. 'colored' folks in the old South

In growing up in the Old South one of my challenges was dealing with racism in my community, in the school, and even at church. My family's attitude toward other races and nationalities was similar to that of Archie Bunker in *All in the Family*. They were raised with the idea that God made all of us a different color for a reason, and that implied separation based on race and ethnic origins.

Like many others, they referred to blacks as "niggers," not because of any deep-down prejudice but more out of habit and tradition. Some folks even said the word developed out of mispronunciation because Southerners had a habit of adding extra "r's" to words — saying taters instead of potatoes and maters instead of tomatoes. Perhaps, out of Negroes came the derogatory word "niggers."

Dad had some black friends who loved to come and "set a spell" with him at the country store or take a walk in the fields with him. They came from up North and regularly visited kinfolk down the road and considered Bud their friend and confidante. He treasured these guys and their visits, but would have drawn the line if I had ever dared date someone that wasn't white.

One of Dad's black friends gave him a humorous item that after many years ended up on the wall at Grandpa's Country Store. We don't know who wrote it but it reflects the disparity in people's attitudes at that time about black people. Here goes:

Sho Nuff

(slang for sure enough)

Dear white fella,

Couple things you should know

When I born, I black

When I grow up, I black

When I go in sun, I black

When I cold, I black

When I scared, I black

When I sick, I black

And when I die, I still black.

You white fella

When you born, you pink

When you grow up, you white

When you go in sun, you red

When you cold, you blue

When you scared, you yellow

When you sick, you green

And when you die, you gray.

And you have the nerve to call me colored?

Remember how we've talked about the THEYs in our lives?

When growing up it was like there was this mysterious group called THEY who ruled our lives and dictated our decisions. What would THEY say? What would THEY think? It felt a lot like Big Brother in the classic novel *1984* by George Orwell... like someone who was always watching us and telling us how we should think, feel, and act.

Well, THEY had a lot to say about the way things were done when it came to colored people.

I never accepted the disrespectful term "nigger" and would never understand why the black people who worked on our farm would not come in the house even when I invited them. An elderly black woman name Henieretta Jackson heard us talking about pizza at the tobacco barn one day and wanted to try some so I told her to come on home with me for dinner break. She walked up to our farm house, and I finally coaxed her into the back porch but that was as far as she would go so I took her out a piece of pizza to the back porch.

For years Henieretta talked about that pizza, but would never come back for more. Mom told me that black folks had always been told to stay in their place and it wasn't in a white person's home.

This distance between blacks and whites showed up in the religious environment at Moore Union Congregational Christian Church. I couldn't understand the hatred and prejudice in what was supposed to be a spiritual place. It seemed to have a lot to do with a certain preacher, Mark Anthony Thomas, a charismatic, butter-wouldn't-melt-in-your-mouth man, who spoke out against colored people. He said it was a sin for black and white folks to worship together, date and, heaven forbid, ever marry. Someone told me if a black and white dared to have "young'uns" they would be born polka dot! Obviously I didn't know any polka-dot kids so I foolishly thought for a long time that I just didn't know any children from inter-racial homes.

One incident that stands out most from my childhood is how this preacher could hate colored people so much. We had just got a box of quarterlies in — those little books we used for three months in our Sunday school classes — and a little black child was on the cover. The preacher went off on some tangent about it being a sin for colored folks to be messing around with white people and their religion. He put those quarterlies right back in the box and sent them to the publisher, refusing to use "anything with a nigger's picture on it."

We didn't use quarterlies for a while and it amazes me that no one questioned the preacher's decision. After all, he was leader of this self-righteous religious group who held the power of condemnation closely to their minds — there was no room for it to be dispelled by forgiveness and love.

This preacher loved my unusual singing voice and invited me to sing duets with him while Peggy Womack played the piano and sang along too. While singing my heart out at church I treasured the messages in the hymns. I believed in the words of a popular song we often sang in Sunday School, "Red and yellow, black and white, they are precious in his sight, Jesus loves the little children of the world."

Meanwhile my school four miles away in a little town called Broadway was not unlike my church, and some teachers held similar views as my family and neighbors. THEY shared information and insights that did not ring true to my soul. I was in high school when segregation was condemned by the government and integration was inflicted on many unwilling participants and created quite a stir in the community.

Just when I was excited about using my singing talent and dramatic ability to participate in more plays and productions they suddenly stopped, and the reason I was given makes no sense to me even today. THEY told me that the colored were going to be coming to our schools and we couldn't be expected to act and sing with the likes of them.

Just when I was looking forward to going on the senior class trip to Washington, D.C. and New York, these outings were banned. THEY told me that we white kids wouldn't be going off with any blacks on any such trips.

In high school history class I wrote a term paper about abolitionism and condemned slavery. I closed with the famous words of Abraham Lincoln, "No man is good enough to rule over another, if he were good enough, he wouldn't want to do it."

I hated modern-day slavery, the way blacks were discriminated against and belittled just because they were black, and held back from getting equal pay for equal work.

THEY complained about "niggers" living off welfare but THEY didn't want to pay them decent wages or give them good jobs.

THEY talked about the old clothes the colored people wore but THEY didn't want them to earn enough money to buy new ones.

THEY criticized them because some black people drove nice cars but lived in "nigger shacks" but THEY didn't bother to understand that others have different priorities.

Race prejudice, righteousness and arrogance...
these were the negative energies that shaped my world,
but as I soaked in these so-called "words to the wise"
I quickly threw them out. I wanted no part of these
people's ideas about coloreds.

If what THEY said was true, perhaps I was
destined to spend eternity engulfed in flames, but right
then my life in Buckhorn community felt a lot like
prison itself. A rage was burning inside me, a wildness
that could not be tamed by deceptive beliefs and
disturbing truths. Surely there had to be something
more than this to life, and I became obsessed about
leaving behind the chains that held others captive.

The free spirit in me longed for wisdom that I
knew had to exist beyond the walls of ignorance and
arrogance. The rebel in me longed for a world where
black and white could worship side by side in a church
focused on bringing a little bit of heaven to everyday
life. The crusader in me believed in a society where
people of all colors could sit in the classroom,
study together, perform in concerts and dramas together,
and take trips together. Somehow there had to be
equality, acceptance and unconditional love in the
world, and I was determined to find it.

"Sandy Lynn"

Chapter 13

Bucking Buckhorn — From a country bumpkin to a city girl

Remember how I told you my nick-name was Sandy but that Mom and Dad hollered "Sandy Lynn" when I didn't live up to their expectations? Now, they would do the same thing to my brother "Jimmy Doyle" and my sister "Mary Carol" but when they yelled "Sandy Lynn" it sounded a lot more ominous.

Mom says I was an angelic child, quiet and shy, who could play alone contentedly for hours with my dolls. Guess she got used to my being the perfect little girl — after all, she told me many times, children should be seen and not heard. As I grew up, however, I began to explore new ideas and do things my way, which didn't set too well with my Mom's controlling personality. She took her role as Mother Hen very seriously and didn't want any of her biddies straying too far from the nest, either physically or mentally.

Meanwhile Dad took a spare-the-rod, spoil-the-child approach with us three "young'uns." When I didn't fit the traditional mold of the model child, he would often lose control, whip my butt, and as his father said to him, he would yell "you'll never amount to anything." Like most country folk Dad expected his children to follow in his footsteps, and he had trouble accepting me because I was "quar" and down-right peculiar with my all my highfalutin notions and "citified" ideas.

To top it off when I'd visit Grandpa at the country store he'd say, "You can't help from being ugly but you could stay at home." Other times he'd comment: "Come on in here and let me put a paper bag over your head...you'd look better that way."

Not understanding his sense of humor I thought I had to be as "ugly as a burnt mole" — a phrase often afforded to the most unattractive of the lot in Buckhorn.

My family just couldn't comprehend a child who preferred reading, writing, singing, dancing, and dramatizing to working on the farm. For me putting in tobacco and shelling peas left much to be desired as a way of life, and I longed to follow the Muse awakening in me. Soon I discovered that while living on this isolated 400-acre farm in "Lettsville" — certainly not close to the music and dancing lessons I craved — I could write. Grandpa's country store was always stocked with shelves of paper tablets and plenty of pencils.

My special private place was the aging '49 Chevrolet in our sunny back yard. Here I parlayed my interest in making up stories about my dolls into creating dramas about bold and beautiful people who lived in exciting places that seemed more interesting to me than participating in a farm family's simple life.

My studio was a secluded spot in the woods next to a seductive pond where I would sit for hours pouring out my poems on paper. The pond's dam served as a suitable stage for my dramatic performances — ranging from heavy-hearted monologues to humor-filled comedy acts. I sang and danced and bowed to my audience of fish, ducks, dogs and cats, who were my allies on my family's farm.

My family? Who were these country folks who talked excitedly about tobacco prices and crop yields?

My girlfriends? Who were these people who chattered constantly about chores and boys?

My boyfriends? Who were these strange creatures who yakked endlessly about ball games and car races?

My family, my classmates, my neighbors...
they laughed when I read my creations aloud.
They howled for days when, at age 15, I told them I
had written my first book titled *I Know What Life Is*.

That's OK, I reconciled, I'd have the last laugh yet.
I'd go to college and become an English teacher and
write books during the summer. Yes, I'd become rich
and famous and marry an important man...we would
have a huge house with rooms full of books —
books I had written and books by great thinkers that
I could read for hours without interruption.
There'd be no one calling out in the middle of a
poem...."Sandy Lynn, you get your self home for
supper."

Yes, I'd show these folks who made fun of me.
I would become an actress, sharing my singing talent
and dramatic ability in theaters all over the world.
I'd change my name to "Alexandra" or "Alexander"
because it would speak of sophistication and exude
worldliness...besides, it would look better on marquees.

When I graduated from high school, second in my class, I carried with me a paper trail of ego tokens — president of the honor society, editor of the school newspaper, winner of the poetry award, and recipient of the American Legion county-wide oratorical award.

Despite all the teasing from other students, they voted me "Most Likely to Succeed" during my senior year at Broadway High School.

When I sang at churches and community events in the area I joked that I was singing "off-Broadway," even though no one had a clue what it meant. As I left Buckhorn and Broadway behind I was determined to "amount to something," and maybe even see my name in lights on the real off-Broadway. I wanted nothing to do with farming and that way of life.

In college the accolades continued...first female student government president, distinguished journalism scholarship winner, campus newspaper editor, most outstanding student award. I was even nominated for homecoming queen so I guess I wasn't "ugly as a burnt mole" after all.

A bout with serious illness during my junior year was the first inkling that life might not play out as I had expected. This crisis led me to an unlady-like distrust of conventional doctors, who had always been held in high esteem by sickly Southern women, and an "unholy" distaste for modern medicine and its frightening side effects.

After a hellish stay in the hospital, a dreadful drug therapy program, and devastating toxemia from experimental hormones, my extracurricular priorities shifted. I became editor of a campus feminist magazine called *SHE*. This traumatic health crisis paved the way for my soapbox years as a crusading holistic health proponent.

Later, while working for a newspaper I wrote a weekly health column called "Natural Living," which was highly praised by my readers and often scorned by mainstream medical practitioners. Popularity of the column led to numerous speaking engagements, publication of a book, *Natural Living: From Stress to Rest* in 1984, and celebrity appearances.

Autograph requests came most often on bad-hair days when I had run over to the grocery store without makeup.

By then I was signing my name "AlexSandra" because my friend Theodora swore she saw this unusual spelling in the sky one day en route to my house. Never doubting her vision I readily changed my public persona to AlexSandra L. Lett and enjoyed pointing out to people that my initials were ALL. And that's who I became...*all* things to *all* people.

"AlexSandra the Great" becomes socialite and public relations executive

My *Natural Living* moment of fame faded away
but I continued to herald other causes and to search
for answers to life's complexities. I published
hundreds of articles and worked on dozens of television
programs and eventually ended up in Raleigh,
the state capital, where I founded and served as
president of a public relations/professional speaking
company. I named it ALL Communications to capitalize
on my initials and reflect a wide range of services —
and true to my pattern, I became *all* things to *all* clients.

Through the years I began to discover that city
life wasn't nearly as exciting as I thought it would be
and that "citified" people certainly weren't any happier
than the country folks I left behind. I also began to
notice that those pastures that seemed so much greener
were colored by the distorted lenses of a wild child
wanting to run free. Life beyond Buckhorn wasn't so
freeing and fulfilling after all.

Maxine Thomas Patterson,
Isabelle Patterson Lett,
Ruby Knight Lett,
and Bettie Lett Garner

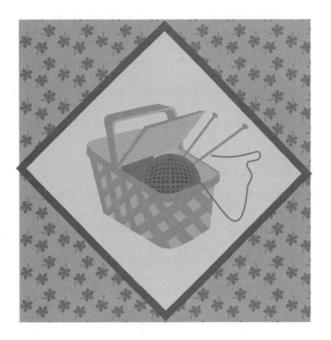

Chapter 14

Life on the farm, wonder woman style

While the men folks were doing back-breaking hard labor on the farm the women were working their fingers to the bone in the house as well as in the fields. In addition to the constant chores related to raising crops, animals and "young'uns"were the never-ending harvesting of produce, canning, freezing, and of course, cooking.

Among the sticks and stones of constant chores were a few seashells and agates, even some flowers. Mom and many farm women relished adding their special touch to projects and bringing their creativity to homemaking.

For example, Mom loved to sew and over the years became an accomplished seamstress. She'd say, "I could sew when I won't no-size and made most of my own clothes while growing up." She especially enjoyed creating clothes for my sister Carolyn and me.

The family would ride up to Stevens Milling Company in Broadway and look through feed sacks in order to pick out which colors and prints we liked best. After the mash for the chickens was poured in the metal barrels, we washed the feed sacks in the ringer washing machine. Then Mom worked her magic by transforming them into dresses, blouses, shorts, pajamas, what-have-you. After starching and ironing the fabrics the creations looked "mighty fine".

Sometimes the material leftover from feed sacks showed up in the linens on our beds. When a dress had "slam-damn" worn out and "weren't" no good for passing on as hand-me-downs anymore, its scraps became folk art in Mama's quilts. Many a tear was shed when we country girls snuggled up in a quilt rich with precious memories of a one-time Easter dress or a former favorite blouse discarded 'cause growing breasts had burst through the seams.

I had a flamboyant flair for the dramatic in dress, and Mom indulged me. In high school I used my work-in-tobacco earnings to buy a "citified" pair of shoes — something unique like a lime green/royal blue combination. Then Dad would take Mom and me to the real fabric store in Sanford and we'd pick out matching green and blue material. I would draw a dress design, and Mom would create a pattern and then whip up the outfit on her sewing machine. Sometimes she even made me a matching pocketbook.

One day I bought an exotic print with red fruit all over it, and Mom and I went all over town looking for matching apple buttons to go down the front. In the middle of the sewing project my sister walked in and said, "Where did you get that wild strawberry dress?" With eyes as big as saucers Mom and I took a closer look at the fabric to discover that, sure enough, the fruits were strawberries and not apples. We went for the fruit bowl effect and used the apple buttons anyway.

Years later, when I sold that sundress with matching pocketbook at a yard sale, there was no price high enough, so I gave it away joyfully to a Mom looking for a special dress for her teenage daughter. Maybe those strawberries are still bringing joy by sprucing up a bed somewhere as a homemade quilt.

My aunt Gladys enjoyed sewing clothes and making quilts from left-over scraps too. She, Mom and some of the ladies from the church and surrounding community would gather often for quilting bees where they helped each other finish their exquisite creations.

The various quilt names reflected life on
the farm, tranquility, marriage, death...all of the major
life events. Women put their life's blood into these
quilts, not only because they were vital for keeping
them warm in cold winters when the fire in stoves
went out at night but because they could express
themselves creatively. In winter when days were
shorter many farm people spent time either in the field,
at the eating table, or in the bed.

It was Gladys' finest hour at many a wedding
shower when the bride opened her gift of a
homemade quilt — a precious present reserved
for only the close of kin and dear of heart.
She often told me she had a quilt with my name on
it but I couldn't have it until I agreed to get hitched.
I reckon someone else is sleeping under that quilt
somewhere.

After Gladys died her heirs treasured finding six
boxes of quilt scraps. Her granddaughter Diane
decided to use the skills she had learned from
Gladys and make good use of the beautiful designs.

She told me, "I went through and took out all the red and navy gingham squares she had cut out. I pieced them together and made a quilt top. It was as if Granny had cut them out herself for me to sew because the proportions and number of squares came out perfectly."

While old quilts represented reality, and each square offered a reminder of clothes long gone, women also used this outlet to express their creativity and to capture precious memories. One spectacular quilt was designed by a neighbor named Cheryl. When her father died, she wanted to do something special in honor of him. While cleaning out his clothes closet she saw all his different flannel shirts. As she folded each shirt, a wonderful memory came back about something her father had done while wearing that particular shirt. That's when she had a great idea. She took the shirts home, cut patches out of each shirt and created a quilt. Because her parents had been married 49 years, she made the quilt using seven squares across and seven squares down, equaling 49. Some of the squares were cut so the shirt pocket was included, offering little pockets to tuck reading glasses or tissue in while curled up in the quilt.

Cheryl says that creating this quilt became a wonderful healing for her, even though she cried some tears during the process. She gave the quilt to her mother as a present for the first Christmas after her father died. Her mother would tell others "this is my most treasured possession. I will keep it on my bed forever, just like I keep him in my heart."

After I had left home Mom made me a wedding ring quilt, so-named because it featured circles interwined with each other. Today I often see quilts featured as examples of artistic expression, whether drapped on beds or hanging on walls, but none will ever be as loved as the wedding ring quilt on my own bed. It will always remind me of a woman who loved me enough to put her life's blood into a gift that will last forever.

*Ruby welcomes everyone to join her
for some "mighty fine" eating*

Chapter 15

Come on by and eat your fill at 'Ruby's Restaurant'

My mother used to say she did more work before most people got up in the morning than they did all day long. When Dad and we three "young'uns" saw the big spread on the breakfast table — freshly-made biscuits, scrambled eggs, ham, sausage, bacon, red-eye gravy, grits, and blackberry and apple jelly — we never doubted her word.

If we kids didn't care for plain milk she'd stir in cocoa to make it chocolate, and if we wanted Coca-Cola for breakfast that was OK too.

Mom — better known as Ruby Lett — believed everyone should have a big breakfast and a wide range of choices. In the summertime she outdid herself, cooking enough food at 4 a.m. to take to the tobacco barn for neighbors pitching in and hired help. Nabs and moon pies from Grandpa's country store were delicious but didn't stick to your ribs like home cooking.

Mom learned about cooking and working hard at a very early age while growing up on a tobacco and cotton farm near Seminole in Harnett County. Like her mother, Mary Ida Yarborough Knight, before her, she followed in the tradition of country cooking — lots of lard or fatback — long before anyone heard of cholesterol in the diet. Mom watched her mother pull out the hide-away shelf on the dish cabinet, use the built-in flour sifter, throw ingredients in a bowl and roll out biscuits.

Mom soon mastered the art of bread-baking, and her heart leaped when her father, Alexander (Bud) Knight, would tell her, "Ruby, this is 'mighty fine' eating." She grew up with two brothers and two sisters and got used to cooking for "a whole mess" of people.

As a farm wife Mom made her mark with her country cooking. She figured out that the key to satisifying the family and the whole community was to fix a wide variety of foods so that everyone could find their favorite at "Ruby's Restaurant."

It certainly seemed like a diner on Sundays when Mom would fix three meats and about six vegetables and also find time to go to Sunday School and Preachin'. It didn't matter who came home with us from church 'cause there was plenty of fixin's for everyone.

Let me tell you about her desserts. Plain Cake was my favorite, similar to Pound Cake, only baked in a flat pan, and served with strawberries, picked, capped and frozen by Mom herself, and topped with fresh cream from Grandpa's cow.

At Christmas Mom made about 20 cakes and would cut them in quarters to give as presents so people got four different kinds on one platter. Mom is the only one in the world who makes a fruitcake that people beg for, even ask for seconds — a light fruitcake and a dark fruitcake (colored by cocoa and enhanced by dark raisins). Whoever came up with the theory that there are only a few fruitcakes in the world that are rotated year to year as Christmas presents because no one wants to eat them has never tasted Mom's.

One time I was sampling all her cakes when she yelled, "Sandy Lynn, if you eat one more piece, you'll pop," and I responded, "pass the platter and stand back!"

Mom's food was always the first to go at neighborhood gatherings and community functions, especially the homecoming spreads at Moore Union Congregational Christian Church, where everyone's first question was, "Where did Ruby put her food?" That's where the feeding line started, and the slow had to settle for second best, which was certainly no hardship 'cause there were County Fair ribbon winners like Aunt Selma's melt in-your-mouth turnip greens, Aunt Alice's fried cornbread, cousin Mary Alice's fresh coconut cake, and the piano player Peggy's tender roast beef and chocolate layer cake.

Much of our food was "born" on our farm, lavish with vegetables and fruit trees, and abundant with animals raised for slaughtering, and a lot of it is still grown there.

When we "young'uns" were shorter than a yardstick, we'd help Mom and Dad with the garden. They felt strongly about growing enough food for all the neighbors in Buckhorn community and beyond. Mom said that she knew someone who knew someone who decided to be selfish one year and just grow enough for her small family. Stinginess breeds disaster, according to Mom, and that year those folks had the worse garden ever and had to take handouts from everyone around. With that in mind we harvested enough beans, peas, sweet corn, tomatoes, and potatoes to feed an army.

We had plenty of company all the time with people beating down the door to grab a chair at our eating table. Well, when the vegetables were ripe for the pickin' folks stomped dead the grass in the back yard, making a bee-line for Lett's farmers' market, just a stone's throw from our kitchen door. Produce, planted with love and nurtured with tender loving care, was free for the pickin'.

In summertime, after tobacco had been primed and put in the barn we ate our fill at "Ruby's Restaurant" and then fell into slumber for a while during the heat of the day. Rising to power again as the sun went down we headed for the garden, and sometimes afterwards, we went straight to Grandpa's country store where we shelled peas and snapped beans while listening to the evening news on the GPCS station...Grandpa Puzie's Country Store, that is. Juicy gossip made the constant chores go faster, and tall tales allowed us to forget all together that we were still "working our fingers to the bone."

While some worked hard and some hardly worked at all, somehow it all got done, but Mom worked the longest and the hardest. And if we complained, watch out for a tongue-lashing because Mom was Wonder Woman and didn't want to hear about our aches and pains and other excuses. She would whip our butts in a minute if we slowed down the production line. She lived in either high gear or broke down, and there "weren't" no in-between. We took breaks only during her many hospital stays, if you can call teary eyes, weary thoughts, worried looks and broken spirits rest.

When feeling spunky Mom always liked to rule the roost. She had a strong personality and liked to be in control, and I was independent and wanted to do things my way, so we clashed often.

After I finished college and was living in Ohio, I came home one summer to visit, and Mom and I were out in the garden picking vegetables. Suddenly she got on her soapbox and started telling me what to do with my life. I cut her off by saying, "The trouble with you Mom is that you run the family, you run the church, and you run the community, and when I come home you think you're going to run me."

She frowned and started to defend herself, and
then realized it was true and started laughing.
We giggled so hard we almost peed in our pants.

Moore Union was Mom's stage for showing off her
many talents. She volunteered her natural business
acumen to serve as secretary-treasurer and never took a
dime for her 40 years of service. She believed in tithing
her time and talent as well as her money. She enjoyed
coordinating the Christmas program because she liked
making things happen, and she'd never admit it,
but she loved telling people what to do. As the audience
applauded the performers and gave kudos to director
Ruby K. Lett, they didn't know that Mom went home
and collapsed for days, having given all she had to give.

Like Wonder Woman, Mom often turned into an
everyday person, and without her cape of courage and
façade of fortitude she was just human like the rest of
us. Behind the persistent, powerful facade Mom was a
puny little lady but it never stopped her from pushing
herself to the limit. Last time we counted Mom had
gone through 40 operations and 50 hospital stays

but sickness couldn't hold a good woman down.
Born to serve, she became the gift that keeps on
giving...even if there "weren't" much left for her.

Even at 80 Mom believes life is ripe for the pickin'
every day. She and Dad still live in the same farmhouse
given to them by Grandpa after Dad returned from
World War II. This year they got a late start on the
garden because of sickness but both of them looked
forward to the first mess of somethin'. Come June there
were peas ready for shelling and eating and freezing.
In July neighbors dropped by for corn-on-the-cob.
Those shucks can be mighty stubborn but the sweetness
inside is worth the wait.

*Mom
holding
Carolyn*

Mom doesn't open "Ruby's Restaurant" so often. She and Dad relish going to uptown Sanford several days a week to dine out. But sometimes on Sundays she rises early and has all the burners fired up and the oven full and even the toaster oven and microwave on. She calls folks and says, "stop by for dinner after church or come on by later for an early supper." The "diner" stays open from noon to bedtime.

So if you're ever coming our way, "set a spell" and eat your fill at "Ruby's Restaurant."

Don't be surprised if Mama puts you to work and Dad acts like the meal is the biggest and best he's ever eaten. I warn you though, Mom and Dad have a whole bunch of kinfolk and four grandchildren and five great-grandchildren who'll also be fighting for the food. You won't be able to get a word in edgeways, but your mouth will be full and your tummy bloated, and that "pert-near" says it all!!!

Chapter 16

Gladys didn't mince words: 'give me snuff, not stuff!'

My first awareness of sin began when I was just a mite — knee-high to a grasshopper. I went across the road to visit Aunt Gladys (pronounced "Glade-ist" more out of habit than any deliberate intention), who was the oldest of Dad's seven sisters and lived with Grandpa.

I was about five years old and was hoping to talk up a storm with Gladys, and she wasn't there but a storm came up anyway. Since I couldn't find her I searched the sewing machine drawers to see if there was something interesting to inspect. Sure enough, there was a pale pink piece of ribbon, edged in lace, and probably left over from one of her sewing projects. I twisted it around my finger and walked to the front porch and realized something big was brewing. As the sky darkened and the wind whistled I heard Mom yelling from our front porch, "Sandy Lynn, you get your butt home."

As the rain poured I became disoriented and dropped the piece of lace, never to be seen again. The next day I searched the area high and low but never found it. Thinking of what I had learned in Sunday School I realized I had taken something without asking permission so I was a thief. Sure, it was just a tiny piece of cloth, nevertheless, I had broken one of the Ten Commandments. This incident bothered me for years, especially because I didn't confess it to Gladys.

It's not that Gladys would have cared about any piece of fabric or any material goods. She liked the simple things in life. She enjoyed making one-of-a-kind gifts and couldn't get excited about giving "store-bought" stuff. Nevertheless her gifts to my sister and me were meaningful though we sometimes traded wares with each other — like the time she gave me a homemade broom decorated with a ribbon to put by a fireplace, and since I didn't have a fireplace, I traded it with Carolyn for the homemade doillies.

Gladys gave a lot but didn't "cotton to" receiving... didn't know how to accept presents from others. In fact, most of the time she didn't even care about birthday and Christmas gifts. Since everybody in the family — Grandpa's children and many grandchildren — gave Grandpa a gift, they automatically bought something for Gladys too. After all, Gladys had returned home to Grandpa's house after a not-so-happy matrimonial adventure and raised both her children, Maxine and Lux, at the old homeplace. She took her Lett name back and became "Grandma Gladys" to the whole family.

Anyway, every Christmas Gladys would get gifts
galore — ranging from bath powder to blouses —
and would pile them in a closet off the living room.
When opening a present she would frown and look at
the giver and say, "What'd you give me that for?
I already got three or four just like it in the 'clawset'"
or "I don't need another set of towels —
I got enough to last me the rest of my life."
She had much rather have snuff than stuff!

Some folks are slow to learn 'cause they'd do the
"same damn thang" next year. While some people
thought Gladys was ungrateful, she had just gotten
tired of hinting about no more presents and decided to
tell the blatant truth. Just shows people didn't listen
'cause the gifts kept coming and Gladys kept
complaining. Often, right after Christmas, I'd be out
there yakking with her and she'd say, "Why don't you
take that good-for-nothing 'thang' home with you?"

Through the years I figured out how to give Gladys something that really mattered to her. Since I was a photography buff and took pictures on special occasions, like birthdays and anniversaries, I started fixing her albums. Every Christmas I'd pull together highlights of the year into a keepsake album. Sometimes I'd add messages on them with hidden meaning....like the time I wrote "They could have danced all night" on a picture of relatives that Gladys said were into hanky-panky. The man was married and had deep pockets, and the woman was a widow. Gladys would look at me and laugh, "When she's with him she thinks she's in high cotton."

Gladys didn't take to uppity stuff of any kind and had no patience with highfalutin people who wanted to own things for the sake of owning them. She became frustrated with siblings and nieces and nephews and cousins twice-removed who wanted her to give them various pieces of furniture from the old homeplace. Her view of antiques could be summed up with the words "old junk."

She told me that "every damn body in the family" wanted the large cherry table in the dining room and she was tired of hearing folks whine about it. One day she got my brother Jimmy to help her move the table out in the yard next to the trash pile.

Within a few minutes a fire was blazing and smoke could be seen for miles around. Oh well, so much for that table! Its ashes traveled hither and yon, and kinfolk knew not to ever mention it again.

From this experience we all learned that Gladys "won't" glad when she was mad!!!

Gladys was a big tall woman with thick black hair and black eyes — she didn't need perms or coloring because her locks could have been used for TV commercials. When growing up I longed to have thick, naturally curly hair like my aunts, and especially Gladys. My blonde hair was fine, and I let it grow to my waist, and my body was thin and petite so I weighed only 105 pounds when I left home.

Gladys keeps cool on the front porch

Even after I went off to college I'd come back and crawl in her lap. She'd hold me like I was still a little girl. We'd laugh — and of course, she'd always mention the time I peed there while watching *I Love Lucy.* We yakked about my writing, my boyfriends, my adventures — all so different from the life she had known on the farm.

For several years I lived in Ohio and one time I drove home 10 hours the day of the Christmas program at Moore Union. As usual I was late and sneaked into the church and sat next to Gladys near the front. She glanced at me and then looked again, realizing it was "Sandy" — she burst into tears and held me tight for a long time. The next day she said the reason she cried was because I had my hair cut — about 12 inches gone! That became another joke between us — that Gladys cried not because she was glad to see me but because she was upset about the missing hair.

One of my fondest memories is the time Gladys told me how much she enjoyed my visits, partly 'cause I didn't wear out my welcome like some folks did.

She never said "I love you" because that was beyond her comfort zone. She never said "you sure did turn out smart" because "purty" words didn't come easy for her. But when I walked into the house, she didn't have to say a word because her black eyes lit up like a child's on Christmas Day.

When I crawled into her lap she held me tighter than necessary and then would pretend to push me away. We were like two peas in a pod, totally different in appearance and worlds part in experience and education, but we were alike in one special way: we loved each other with all our hearts.

During Grandpa's final years Gladys took care of him. They put a bed in the den where he lay and visitors came often. He loved Gladys' plain cake better than anything in the world, and she fixed him one every few days. If he wanted just plain cake and Coca-Cola for lunch then that was what he got. She dared anyone to mention fresh vegetables or a better diet. "He's 88 years old and has done just fine eating any damned thing he pleased," she'd say.

After Grandpa died in 1977 Gladys wanted to get out more so she started driving his car. She tried to get a driver's license but couldn't figure out how to answer the questions on the written test. That didn't stop her. She cruised anywhere she pleased, and when folks warned her about getting in trouble driving without a license, she'd say, "Who's gonna stop an old lady like me?"

Gladys and Grandpa were partners in crime when it came to living just the way they wanted to with little regard for the good opinion of others.

Years after Gladys died my first column about Grandpa and the Letts was published on her birthday, April 7, 2000. I sent copies to her children to remind them of our good times together. Among my fondest memories of Aunt Gladys is sitting in her big lap, feeling very safe and very loved!!!

Chapter 17

Party line — 'Twas a party for listeners-in and passersby

The telephone came to Grandpa's house in Buckhorn too late to help with firing the flame of my first love affair in fifth grade. For years I blamed lack of communication for my lost love because when Gerald Hunter and I parted ways for summer break I couldn't compete with the girls he could ring up on the phone.

Years later this problem persisted when suitors couldn't pursue me as readily because I lacked the missing ingredient for being a popular girl. While Grandpa was suspicious of fancy gadgets and modern-day conveniences, that attitude quadrupled when it came to Dad because he couldn't see any point in any of it. Even though Amish in orientation, the Letts did have electricity, and thanks to Aunt Gladys, who put her foot down now and then, got a phone for her and Grandpa.

Fortunately for me I was cute and sweet enough that some guys found it worth the effort to track me down under Grandpa's name in the telephone book. Whenever Tom, Dick or Harry called Gladys would yell from the front porch, "Your beau's on the phone," and I'd go running. If I missed the call she'd take a number, and I'd call back. (This was before *The Rules* guidebook for girls, mind you!)

Finally Mom talked Dad into getting a telephone, and we were on the same party line with Gladys, which meant if she was using the phone we couldn't and vice-versa. This also meant that we could listen into each other's conversations. Well, the *Bible* didn't say anything about eaves-dropping so my sister and I felt obligated to stay abreast of the latest gossip by listening to Gladys tell So-and-So who was messing around with whom.

The telephone was definitely an instrument destined to spread good and evil far beyond the confines of Buckhorn. Well, what is good for the goose is good for the gander! Gladys began to entertain herself by listening in on my conversings with different gals and guys from high school. She tried to be quiet but I could hear her steady breathing through the receiver, and even when I'd say, "Someone is listening in," she'd still hang on for dear life. After all, these calls were usually made well past soap opera time, often after supper, and were obviously more interesting than some of her TV shows.

Once while in the middle of a flirty, romantic, teasing conversation with a suitor named Jerry, Gladys lost control of her senses and piped in, "You think you're sparkin' don't you?" Another time she mumbled, "You ain't big enough to be courtin' on the phone."

I responded, "Well, yes, Gladys I was trying to court but it's kinda hard to do so when there's an uninvited chaperone on the phone." This time she heaved and then quickly hung up.

The phone was my favorite invention because suddenly I could do homework with classmates, talk forever about basketball games with Patricia, Elizabeth and Barbara, and yak endlessly about boys with Gaye.

Fighting for the phone became commonplace in our home, especially since Mom was secretary-treasurer of the church and talked tirelessly to members about everything from the cemetery fund to sinful fun among the not-so-holy. If there was one thing that got nailed into my brain at home as well as at Grandpa's house and country store, it was that juicy gossip superseded all other activities. Even among God-fearing Christians who supposedly learned at church not to speak or spread ill will, talking about the neighbors ranked high on the list of favorite pastimes. And if God didn't want folks to talk about others then why did God invent the telephone?

Yes, wagging tongues want to know! Inquiring minds want to learn who said what to whom and when and under what circumstances.

That is when my view of life as being like a soap opera began — and despite years of education and many other experiences while outing and abouting — I learned to create craziness like the soap stars as a natural part of my daily drama.

After all, the colorful characters in Buckhorn thrived on talking about such things as affairs and illnesses and even weather reports shared day in and day out on the telephone.

But their trials and tribulations paled in comparison
to the traumas watched in awe on television sets,
but nevertheless everything was big news by the time it
passed through the multiple tellings on the telephone.
I learned one lesson well — if life wasn't a soap opera
it "weren't" no life at all!

While friendships were formed and fed through
daily updates on the phone sometimes, it didn't matter
a whole lot who was on the other end of the line —
as long as each could get in a word edgewise.
My cousin Mary Alice Crissman told me that her Mom,
Bettie Lett, once dialed a wrong number and
commenced to talking to the unknown person, got her
name, and a half-hour later was still yakking with
this fast friend. Come to find out, they had a lot in
common and to their delight discovered a whole
new group of folks who were breaking the
Ten Commandments left and right!

Living in different places where social mores varied, I was always surprised to return home and realize how important the telephone was in my mom's life. Whether she was participating in the gossip chain or directing the Christmas program at church, she thrived on communication and connection offered by the phone. I was constantly surprised at the way she called the same folks everyday and talked like they hadn't seen each other in months.

Years later when I came home for a while and worked as lifestyles editor of *The Sanford Herald* newspaper I was amused that I could so easily get sucked into her daily phone ritual. Mom felt neglected if I didn't call her every day and report the news, no matter how trivial it might be. What shocked me even more is that I began to follow in her footsteps and created co-dependent relationships with friends who fully expected me to call them several times a week. Even today I am a phone addict, preferring to often call and chat with family and friends rather than go to the trouble of getting dressed and visit in person.

Obviously party lines are a thing of the past, but the fascination with the telephone increases. If Grandpa and Gladys knew how much us "young'uns" depended on car phones and "cell" connections these days, they'd roll over in their graves. They'd also be jealous! Surely, up there in heaven, juicy gossip isn't high on the list of daily activities. But just hold on, Grandpa and Gladys, any day now, someone's going to invent a phone with reception good enough to reach the Big Blue Yonder. Earth calling God! People phoning angels! There's a party going on in the Universe — sinners and saints yakking up a storm. Juicy gossip and tall tales from Grandpa's country store will be riding the air waves with many a folk "setting a spell" and spreading the news.

Still it just won't be the same as being there...no phone conversation can ever compare to hearing the country folk wag their tongues and seeing them wave their arms while telling their saucy stories at Grandpa's country store!

Chapter 18

'Rise and shine,' Bud Lett...
my father, my friend

When growing up in the 1950s I confess that I began
to compare my Dad to other father figures I watched
on our newest gadget, the television set. Now Dad
was certainly not like Mr. Suit and Tie Jim Anderson
(played by Robert Young) on *Father Knows Best*.

For one thing Dad hated Sunday go-to-meeting clothes,
and my Mom — wearing her fancy frock —
had to yell "Puzie Doyle, you get those overalls off"
more often than not on Sunday mornings.
Dad reluctantly donned his suit and cranked up the
'49 Chevrolet, and Mom and we three "young'uns"
crawled in. Mom made sure we all looked like angels
in our homemade outfits because folks at Moore Union
Congregational Christian Church expected everyone
to dress "mighty fine" each week for Sunday School
and preachin'. Church was the house of the Lord
and we showed our respect to God by coming clean
and looking good.

   Dad was an unusually handsome rascal,
"pert-near" the best looking man in the Buckhorn
community of Lee County. He could put Rock Hudson
to shame when he had his hair slicked back and his
finest clothes on, but he didn't like dressing up.
He felt his best when he was wearing navy blue
overalls and a short-sleeved shirt, which showed off his
year-round farmers' tan, brown from the elbow down.
He often wore a cap featuring the names of various
businesses in the area.

Most days Dad was a lot like Jed Clampett (played by Buddy Ebsen) on *The Beverly Hillbillies*, expressing confusion about everything different in modern society. He avoided progress like the plague, relishing the mule-drawn sleds bringing tobacco to the barn instead of "wasting money on new fangled contraptions" like tractors and farm equipment. Dad would have been just as happy without electricity. He enjoyed taking a soak in the big tin tub outdoors in the summer and doing a bird bath almost daily indoors during chilly weather. Like his father Puzie before him he viewed fancy gadgets with suspicion, saying we did just fine before plumbing, so why do we need it now?

When hanging out at Grandpa's country store where the men talked about tobacco for hours instead of whispering loudly about juicy gossip, I often wondered if these people were really trying to drive me crazy. I was proud however, that Dad's tobacco usually sold better than anyone else's. I wonder now if it had anything to do with how he used to walk in the tobacco fields in late afternoon and check for worms and weeds and any aliens attacking his babies.

*Bud Lett is proud of growing produce
like this large sweet potato*

Mom would swear that when she worried about
Dad being gone so long and went to fetch him he
would be walking down those tobacco rows yakking
up a storm and laughing like he was surrounded by a
crowd of people. She always asked who he was talking
to and what he was saying but he never devulged a
thing. Perhaps Dad was communing with Mother Nature
long before scientists proved that talking to plants made
them grow larger and stay healthier.

Dad liked things that came naturally and easily,
like music. Everyone said he could play music by ear.
He had never been trained but could hear a song and
then pick out the notes on his guitar and play it like he
had practiced for weeks.

My favorite times with Dad related to our mutual
love for music. Folks said I had the voice of an angel,
should become a singer but Dad didn't take to that
because that would mean me traveling far and wide.
However, he did encourage me to help him learn to
play his favorite songs.

On Sunday afternoons after eating ourselves into fat slumber he'd ask my sister, Carolyn, and me to sing the hymns from church service over and over again so he could pick out the notes on the guitar. His favorite song was "Dust on the Bible" about a preacher who came to a home one day and asked to see the Good Book, and when the folks gave it to him, it was covered with dust from lack of use. Dad and I would sing, "Dust on the Bible, dust on the Holy Word" until we grew hoarse.

Dad was shy about performing in public, would never even sing in the choir at Moore Union, but he would play up a storm with that guitar. Neighbors would drop by to hear him and sometimes they'd sneak in and listen quietly from another room when he was letting it all hang out. If he found them out he'd calm down and stick to the regulars.

During childhood my pet peeve about Dad also related to music because he'd come into my bedroom way too early in the morning and holler "rise and shine" and then break into song so loud I'd bolt out of bed like greased lightning. Nothing like having a thunderstorm wake you up every day!

The whole world was Bud Lett's stage.
Dad was a comedian — his humor was contagious,
and he'd laugh hysterically at himself. Juicy gossip
didn't excite him but he loved to tell tall tales and
would run a joke in the ground. He never tired of
telling the same crazy stories and funny jokes, and
we never tired of hearing them.

Dad's sense of humor paid off when dealing with the
family. Mom was sick a lot and could be "ill as a
hornet." Each summer Mom and Dad and we
"younguns" labored long and hard, puttin' in tobacco
and shucking corn, shelling peas and snapping beans
for canning and freezing. To Dad vegetables and fruits
were diamonds in the rough. After weeks of blanching
and bagging Mom was bone tired and hated the sight
of anything fresh. One day in early fall Dad went
out in the garden and came in the house showing
Mom the various "jewels" still shining in his treasure
chest. Mom was in one of her "ill" moods and yelled
at Dad, "Get those 'thangs' out of here." Dad's
excitment seemed to fade, and then he looked at me
and winked. He pointed his finger at Mom and started
singing, "You need to have a little talk with Jesus."

I laughed so hard I fell out of the kitchen chair.
Mom gave us a mean-as-a-snake look, then caught the
magic of the moment and let loose with a bunch of
giggles. The shared laughter melted Mom's fatigue
like sun on snow.

Surely it was Dad's sense of humor along with his
constant activity that kept him healthy and happy.
We were quite surprised when at 80 he had to be rushed
to the emergency room in March 2000. Dad almost
died and while sitting by his bedside in the hospital,
watching him slip farther away, I knew I was not ready
to let him go. We had become friends, having set aside
our differences in the name of unconditional love and
acceptance. For a while he was so sick and drugged
he didn't know most people but he always recognized
Mom and me. When everyone else had given up on
trying to shave him I soaped his face and mowed the
prickly hairs off with a razor. To ease his confusion I
teased him playfully, "you're a good-looking man."
He looked at my nephew Billy nearby and said,
"that's a bunch of bull." As his sentences became less
coherent I wondered if I had lost Dad forever.

One day I came to the hospital, learned he had
not slept a wink, and he refused to eat and walk for
the 10th day in a row. I put my foot down with the
nurses, forbade them to give him any more drugs!
As the medicines wore off the nurses thought a miracle
had happened overnight. Dad awoke, asked for
breakfast, walked down the hall, and made such a
remarkable recovery that the doctor sent him home that
day instead of the nursing care facility already booked.

Dad had come back to us. Once home, he got well
so quickly he decided to set out a garden, even though
Mom was concerned that taking care of a garden
would be too much. I reminded her that growing
vegetables and fruits would be the most healing thing
Dad could do. When we celebrated Dad's 81st birthday
on April 2, 2000 and his and Mom's 58th anniversary
it was a glory to behold his joy at being surrounded
by his family. It was a scene right out of *The Waltons*.

For a few more summers I'm looking forward to "setting a spell" with Dad and Mom under the big pecan tree in the back yard while shelling peas, snapping beans, shucking corn, and eating tomatoes right off the vine. After all, Dad and I have a lot to catch up on...as friends always do.

Just recently I brought him a pack of windmill cookies that tasted just like the two-for-a-penny ones we used to eat at Grandpa's country store. He devoured them. When I was leaving he gave me a $20 bill to fill up my car with gas, acting like I was still in college. It was like we were starting all over, him wanting to take care of me his way and my finally letting him. We've opened our hearts to the best each has to offer, and finally we've come home to each other, this time to stay...

"Rise and shine," Bud Lett, my father, my friend.

Chapter 19

'King George'— Ruler of hearts and champion of corn

When I was a "young'un" my favorite thing in the whole world was animals. Quite frankly I liked them better than my family and friends because animals didn't make me feel different and didn't tease me about being "quar."

One thing's for sure, the animals never taunted like the country folks with comments like "Sandy Lynn, you must be crazy sitting in that car writing fancy stuff. You don't got nothing to say." When I would disappear for hours and Mom would finally find me doing my one-woman show on the pond's dam in the woods for my audience of fish, ducks, cats and dogs, she would have a hissy-fit, "Sandy Lynn, you're going to be the death of me."

For the most part I hated farm chores because when left to my own devices, I preferred reading, writing, studying and reflecting. There was one obligation I enjoyed — it was feeding the farm animals. We communicated with each other, and they loved me unconditionally. Nothing was wasted on our farm because I appointed myself the "queen of leftovers." Meat scraps went to the dogs and cats, discarded vegetables to the chickens, and everything else edible to the hogs.

We raised chickens and hogs for food and had mules for pulling the tobacco sleds, and our many cats and dogs propagated like flies. If an animal got sick he died, if in pain, Grandpa Puzie or my brother Jimmy would shoot him. Like me, Daddy was tender-hearted and couldn't hurt a flea. Maybe it had something to do with seeing all that killing during World War II.

Animals were my closest and constant companions, and nothing touched my heart like a new litter of kittens. Eyes closed they could not see the child who whispered sweet-nothings in their ears but they grew up to worship me. My favorite cat was named George, who was a gift from a neighbor when I was about 11 years old. At first he was like a wild tiger, hiding in the tall pines in our yard or disappearing in the attic space. Once we opened our hearts to each other there was no turning back.

Dad said he would never allow a cat in the house, but eventually he succumbed to George's charms. Dad, wearing his overalls and a short-sleeved shirt, would nonchalantly walk into the house with a sneaky look on his face. George would catch the scent and awake from his nap with a wild rush.

He would run up Dad's overalls and out his arm where, sure enough, Dad had a dead mouse hiding in his hand!

When Mom scrambled eggs in the morning she fixed a plate for George too. He stayed out all night, came in loudly begging for grub, and got his heart's desires. After devouring his breakfast George would come to my bedroom and tenderly put his paws on my eyelids, prodding me to snuggle with him before I joined the family at the breakfast table. As soon as I was up he crawled into the warm spot in the bed while reveling in my scent.

Later after we "young'uns" were on the school bus, Mom would make up my bed, leaving a big lump in the middle where George rested for hours. Visiting neighbors finally quit asking about the strange hump on Sandy's bed. Everyone knew that George roamed by night and slept by day in his soul mate's bed.

George was my best friend in the whole wide world. Eventually we came to call him "King George" because he ruled the roost at our house.

One of the things that George liked best was eating corn on the cob. He loved the buttery sweetness and eventually discovered that it came from the nearby garden. He would often come to the house and cry until someone followed him to the row of corn and shuck him some for an afternoon snack. He liked it raw as well as cooked.

One summer day we decided to play a trick on George who loved to attend our corn-shuckings and eat until he fell over in sweet slumber. He was resting peacefully on my bed when he heard chattering, shucking, silking, cutting and putting in pots in preparation for freezing. He peeped out the window to see that we were having a party and he hadn't been invited. He put all four paws on the screen and yelled loudly. We all knew what he was saying, "Let me out and give me some corn," but we wouldn't. He continued to yelp and cry, ran back and forth from front door to back, begging for release. When we finally let him join us he broke his record and gobbled down three ears of corn.

George was a fat cat that night, and we were a happy family — having laughed loud and long. We agreed on one thing: King George was our beloved teacher, the ruler that brought our hearts together in perfect harmony under the same roof.

Now George could be a wild child. He was an "unfixed" Tom Cat who took his maleness seriously, going off for days in pursuit of females in heat for miles around. He would come back skinny from too much wooing and too little feeding, and we would lavish him with treats.

Once George stayed gone for three weeks, and the ache in my heart grew deeper with every passing day. We feared he had ventured too far, maybe gotten killed by a rival male, or just lost his way. Then one night while watching TV we heard a faint cry from the front porch. Sure enough, it was George, or what was left of him, down to skin and bones and sporting a deep cut on his head. We smothered him with kisses and hugs, and Mom went to the kitchen and fixed one of his favorite meals — scrambled eggs. That night he slept in my bed with me, and for both of us the healing began.

The cat population grew rapidly at our house as George spawned a long line of descendants. Among his many mistresses was Alexander. The highlight of my childhood days was when Alexander and George's first litter of kittens was born. Mom kept moving them out to the barn, but within an hour, Alexander would have all three of them nesting in the back porch. Eventually Mom won but I helped Alexander by sneaking the babies inside the house often for food and fun. I would put the black and white "furballs" on the living room floor and play for hours.

Animals were among my greatest joys during childhood...they were the gifts that kept on giving. When I set myself apart as the "wise writer," and family and friends called me "weird," animals loved me above all else because I shared with them my heart, my soul. Finally I've learned to do that with people and have figured out that folks, like animals, all want the same thing: someone to love.

Jimmy, Carolyn and "Sandy Lynn"

Chapter 20

Holidays on the farm —
Passing on the greatest gifts

When Grandpa and Grandpa were raising nine children in the big farmhouse, scraping by was a way of life so when the holidays came it was slim pickins'. Of course, the focus then was totally on the religious significance so buying "thangs" was not a priority. "The Christmas season kinda started with Thanksgiving when we'd take the time to be grateful for what we had," Grandpa said.

"We'd put on the biggest spread of the year and eat pumpkin pie until we were so full we'd all have to take a cat nap," he told me.

Later the "young'uns" would get out in the yard and play ball or hide and go seek when it was warm enough. If the weather was too chilly, the family would gather around the potbellied stove and do what they did best — tell stories about the year and tease each other. Sometimes they'd play card games or checkers.

Thanksgiving signified the beginning of a time when all the children started their various projects, such as sewing aprons, knitting doillies, making potholders, baking breads and cakes, and carving pipe handles and whistles, as presents to each other.
There wasn't enough time and money to give 11 gifts to everyone so the children created something special for their Mom — like a apron or a potholder. For their Dad it might be an new pipe, knife handle or scarf.

The parents made a special trip to the store to get apples, oranges, grapes and hard candy. Each child got either a pair of socks or pair of gloves, whichever they needed most. There weren't any fancy stockings hanging over the fireboard but plain boxes under the Christmas tree, usually shoe boxes or a container about that size.

The holiday season was kicked off each year when Grandpa would take the "young'uns" on a journey, more exciting than any trip to a foreign country. It was the annual ritual of searching for the perfect tree, always cedar, to put up in the living room. While the boys made a stand for holding the tree, the girls fixed popcorn in a big pot and started stringing it with fish twine, alternating the popcorn with cranberries to create a red and white chain that circled the tree.

This was before electricity, mind you, so they placed oil lights near the tree so everyone could see the masterpiece. One year Grandpa splurged on real candles that were attached to the branches of the tree. "It was a heavenly sight," he said.

"We had to be mighty careful not to burn the branches and set a fire."

The Christmas season was filled with activities around the church and community. The preacher did a couple of special sermons. Soloists showed off their talents and the choir sang the traditional holiday songs. The group also went on a special outing — they got on the back of a wagon and went up and down the road singing hymns and Christmas carols.

"We always stayed longer at the shut-ins," Grandpa said.

Some folks appreciated the visit so much they'd give the singers treats like pecans from the yard or sweet potatoes straight from the oven.

As my Dad grew up he and Mom took on many of the customs of their family and kept Christmas focused on making practical presents for each other and the "young'uns." Through the years as we attended school and learned about what other kids were getting for

Christmas our wish lists grew longer. The highlight of the season for my sister and me was the day the Scars catalog arrived. We looked at it together, and she'd choose an item from one side of the page and I'll salivate over something on the other side.

Back then my brother would want one item like a wagon and be happy as a lark if he received that and some clothes. One time he got a black and white bicycle, which my sister also learned to ride, and eventually it was passed on down to me as my legs grew long enough to touch the pedals.

One year I longed for a watch, and Mom and Dad gave me one that had Cinderella on the front. I was delighted until I took it to school, and my friend Ava told everyone it was cheap. She even came back the next day with a copy of the ad showing the price of it. For years Ava's antics taught me a lot about shame and fired my desire to want more "thangs" that cost a lot of money, but that's another story for another day!

Meanwhile on the farm Christmas became more and more important through the years as we allowed sales catalogs and trips to town to make us three "young'uns" ask for more "thangs." Our commercial desires didn't influence Mom and Dad one bit — they continued to focus on Christmas as being the birthday of Jesus Christ and reminded us often that the baby Jesus was given special gifts from the three Wise Men. They also said if a manger was good enough for Jesus, a farmhouse was good enough for us.

While participating in special services at church during the holidays we also collected good used things to take to poor people in the neighborhood. Our church started a treat giveaway where after the big Christmas program a Santa Claus would drop by and give everyone who attended a paper bag containing several fruits, a few nuts, a box of raisins, and some hard candy. We kids thought we had died and gone to heaven when we received this and over the next days traded our loot with each other and relished the constant treats. A group from the church took these treat bags to shut-ins and sick folks and also poor people to add some holiday cheer.

Through the years the highlight of Christmas was getting involved with Mom's baking projects. We started the holiday ritual with my sister and I helping her make the sugar cookies — comprised of flour, butter, eggs, and sugar. The dough was rolled out flat on white cloths, and we cut it into different designs and put them on a baking pan. To this day there is nothing that tastes better than old-fashioned sugar cookies, sometimes called tea cakes. We didn't add decorations because these plain cookies were "mighty fine" eating. What was equally good was the raw batter that my sister and I ate together with two spoons, fighting each other for the sweet taste. Eventually one of us won the prize of licking out the bowl.

Mom's desserts became so well-known that everyone wanted some. She would bake about 20 cakes in December, and arrange them into creative combinations of 1/4 red velvet, 1/4 carrot cake, 1/4 German chocolate, and 1/4 fruit cake. Only the most special of friends and family received this Ruby Cake, as we came to call it.

Meanwhile Dad did his share. While Mom was the queen of cooking he was the king of pecans — pronounced "pee-cons." He'd pick out pecans night after night so she'd have plenty of nuts for her baking needs. Eventually our largest pecan tree produced enough for us to package some in plastic bags and give them as Christmas presents. Our holiday season officially started on Thanksgiving Day when we'd all gather around the big pecan tree in the back yard and pick up nuts and put them in buckets in the back porch. One of Dad's favorite gifts was the fancy nut-cracker we gave him one year for Christmas and even to this day he enjoys picking out pecans, and we don't mind one bit.

Last year they harvested about 40 pounds of pecans from the same tree in the back yard, and meanwhile many other trees are increasing their yields. I was teasing Dad recently that the rate the trees are growing he'll have a full-time job picking out pecans by the time he's 90.

Looking back over the half-century I've known my Mom and Dad I now understand why they didn't let us kids get caught up in the commercialism of Christmas.

They were wise enough to know that there were greater
gifts to pass on — though we "young'uns" didn't
always appreciate them at the time. Now that we're
older and finally wiser, we know that what we remember
most are the little things — like Dad playing the guitar
with us while we sang "Angels We Have Heard on
High" and Mom letting us lick the cookie batter bowl.
We recall sitting around the kitchen table and sampling
Mom's different cakes and watching Dad tasting every
one twice, trying to decide which one was the best.
I remember Mom and Dad holding each other close,
and us three children gathering around them.

We learned that the best presents are those that last
day in and day out, not the "thangs" that strike our
fancy for a while, but the everyday blessings that touch
our hearts. Sometimes it shows up as a pecan just
picked from the shell or cookies fresh from the oven,
sometimes it's a song played on the guitar, sometimes
it's a smile that comes from somebody's core.
The message of Christmas has always been about the
birth of love...God's gift to a world that constantly needs
reminding that there's only one thing that matters most
every day, and that is loving each other.

On August 25, 2000, Bettie and Wes Lett
celebrated their 72nd anniversary

Chapter 21

Wes and Bettie Lett —
72 years of sharing the good life

Everyday life in rural North Carolina during the Roaring Twenties varied dramatically from the high life in the big city. The courtship of Wes Lett and Bettie Lanier, for example, could not compare to the fickleness and craziness of the era's most famous couple, F. Scott Fitzgerald and Zelda.

Commitment was a word rarely used in the Buckhorn community because it was assumed to be a core value among God-fearing Christians. When a country man and woman stood before the magistrate, justice of the peace or preacher to say "for better or for worse," they meant it.

On Saturday, August 25, 1928, Wes and Bettie spoke their vows at the home of a magistrate, Charlie Lloyd, on Avent Ferry Road, just a few miles from Lett's homeplace. Back then no one cared about fancy white gowns — Bettie wore a freshly-sewed, homemade light brown frock trimmed in dark brown. On the front porch there were pumpkins fresh from the field instead of store bought flowers.

After the morning ceremony the couple jumped excitedly in Wes' brand spanking new 1928 Ford roadster with a rumble seat, and headed for a dinner on-the-grounds feast at Holly Springs Baptist Church near Broadway. Later they traveled to White Lake about two hours away where they swam and "enjoyed being together," Bettie said. For supper they ate hot dogs that cost five cents each.

The couple spent their wedding night at Wes' parents home where they discovered a bell tied under the bed as a joke — a prank to alert others in case they indulged in any moving around other than sleeping!

Wes said he first "took a fancy" to Bettie when he met her and her parents, Herbert and Alice Lanier, at Moore Union Congregational Christian Church. One special Sunday afternoon after church Bettie had fixed a box lunch for a fund-raising event, because whoever placed the highest bid got to eat with the cook too. Wes had to beat out another suitor by coming up with more money in order to have lunch with the woman he loved. Meanwhile, the church used the proceeds to buy a new piano.

One time when they played a popular game called Spin the Bottle with friends, the bottle pointed to Bettie, who could choose whether to hug, kiss, or hug and kiss Wes. She chose the latter, and the magic exploded.

Bettie said, "When Wes was going with me he asked, 'Do you love me enough to marry me?,' and I replied, 'Are you asking me?,' and he said, 'Yes.'"

"I told him I needed a week to study about it, and when I talked to my Mom, she expressed concern because those Lett boys like to nip the bottle."

"When I talked to Wes about my Mom's comment he promised me if I'd marry him he'd never drink again," she said. "When I relayed this to Mom she told me, 'A man's promise is just as easily broken as a pie crust.'"

Bettie said she liked Wes' big blue eyes and his curly hair and relished riding around in his new car, but what really mattered most was that she felt comfortable being with him. She soon "fell head over hills" in love with him and couldn't imagine life without him.

They married when Bettie was 19 and Wes had just turned 24 two days before. About 10 months later their first child, a baby girl, was stillborn. "That was the worst day of my life and the saddest time of our marriage," she said.

Six years later Mary Alice arrived, and this was the happiest day of the couple's life. "Mary Alice was always a joy and continues to be the best daughter anyone could ever have," Bettie said. About seven years passed, and then a son was born, Herbert Lee.

Bettie stayed home with the children while they were growing up and then was employed as a sales clerk for 25 years at a department store in downtown Sanford. After leaving there she worked for two years in the cafeteria at Broadway School where her grandchildren were students.

Wes and Bettie opened their home to Herbert's children, Terry and Michelle, for many years, and opened their hearts to their four step-grandchildren David, Louise, Jane and Kim when Mary Alice married Nathan Crissman 36 years ago.

The couple has always lived on land Wes was given by his parents, Edd and Ida Womack Lett, near Lett's Landing. Wes was named for his grandfather, John Wesley, born in 1852, who had married M. Arnettie Thomas, and inherited part of the original Lett settlement.

Like his father before him Wes loved the land. Following in the footsteps of his family, Wes became a farmer, growing lots of cotton and expanding into tobacco as the main money crop. He also focused on raising cattle and hogs.

Today Wes has curtailed farming and cut back on chores but, "I never saw any reason to retire," he said. Several times a year he performs a ritual — he moves his herd of Black Angus cows down Buckhorn Road to a different pasture for better grazing. "I do this on Sunday morning when there isn't much traffic," he said. With the help of Nathan, Wes still takes the cows to market in Siler City once a year.

The cows partake of an ever-flowing spring near the house. This spring has been providing fresh water to the Lett descendents for many generations. Wes and Bettie don't need a well but use a pump to access water from the spring. "We used to have to carry the water up the hill about 200 feet but now the pump does that," he said.

Now Wes spends his days gathering garden produce and taking care of his cows. He enjoys jumping on his tractor and mowing pastures. He likes to "set a spell" each day at the gate to the river just below the house he and Bettie have shared for 70 years. It's a small house filled with a large amount of love, blessed with memories of children and laughter.

Progress has not taken away the things that matter most to Bettie and Wes Lett, as they relish the visits of family members and friends who live nearby, and of grandchildren and great-grandchildren.

On August 23, 2000, Wes noted his 96th birthday, and on August 25, the couple celebrated their 72nd anniversary. They had a double reason to be grateful. "We've been very lucky to have each other all these years, " Bettie said.

For several days folks dropped by to wish Wes a happy birthday. He didn't want a party but he didn't turn away a big cake to share with others.
"I just enjoy being with family and friends," he said.

Today Mary Alice, who retired as Lee County Veterans Service Officer, and Nathan, former Lee County Tax Administrator, live next door on the farm and help take care of Bettie and Wes. Herbert resides in Wilmington and owns the *Carolina Beach/Kure Beach Weekly News*, where my first column on the Letts was featured in April 2000.

Life along the Cape Fear River has changed dramatically but colorful characters such as Wes and Bettie Lett stay the same. Their property is like a postcard, its beauty frozen in time with its rustic buildings from another era.

At 96 Wes doesn't move quite as swiftly as he used to, but there's a twinkle in his blue eyes and a smile on his lips. At 92 Bettie has trouble seeing due to a degenerative eye disease so she can't read anymore, but there's still a sense of joy in her voice, especially when she talks about the good old days. What she misses most is attending services at Moore Union where she taught Sunday School for 62 years. "I usually taught young people, but one time I had an adult class, and Wes was in it," she said. "That was one time he really listened to everything I said."

After 72 years of commitment, Bettie says marriage is about putting the other person's needs first, and caring for each other in sickness as well as in health. Marriage isn't about "purty words and fancy phrases," she noted, "but about loving another person with all your heart 'til death do us part."

Chapter 22

Gilbert, 'Mr. Rolls Royce,' amounts to something big in the city

When we were growing up we were told over
and over that it was easier for a rich man to pass
through the eye of a needle than to get to Heaven.
Poverty was a virtue, THEY said, and if we coveted
"citified" possessions then we were probably possessed
by the Devil himself. Religion was about loving
the Lord and others, living by the Good Book, and
raising "young'uns" in the way of righteousness.

Anything else was just a wayward way of worshiping Satan's gold.

However, through the years as some of the kinfolk accumulated elaborate houses, fancy cars and big companies, the family began to look at money differently — especially when one of our own became available to loan money for buying houses, starting businesses, and writing big checks to the home church.

That's what happened with my Dad's only brother Gilbert and nary a soul in the family, Buckhorn community or throughout the entire state of North Carolina would dare question Uncle Gilbert's ability to walk through the eye of that needle! In fact, Gilbert would probably be driving his Rolls Royce straight through the pearly gates when Judgment Day came.

Now, let me tell you about Gilbert. He was born in August 1924, the seventh child of Captain Puzie and Verta in the house at Daniels Creek. It was said back then that the seventh child had special powers and one being the gift of divination — or using a hickory stick to find a vein of water under the ground. This came in mighty handy before a well was dug. Sure enough, Gilbert could do just that— and as it turned out this was just one of his many talents.

Gilbert was nicknamed "Shine" because of his bright blonde hair. Perhaps this was a sign that he was a golden child, destined to become a shining star. It was hard for Gilbert to shine on the farm though because he just couldn't seem to please Grandpa, not that anyone could, mind you.

Take cotton, for instance, Gilbert just didn't "cotton to" it all. "My brother and every one of my sisters picked 200 pounds a day, and I worked just as hard but only got half that much," Gilbert said.

Back then schooling was not at the top of the list for farm families, but the local boys and girls went to a two-room schoolhouse called Hickory Level to learn to read and write. They walked a mile there and back. After Gilbert finished first grade, this country school was annexed into the school system and the teacher made him repeat first grade to catch up with the other kids from the bigger and better school. Later he was held back another grade which put him in the same room with his sister Selma. "That shed a bad light on my life, making me a second class student," he admitted.

That incident was the straw that broke the camel's back for Gilbert — and he dropped out of school at age 14 and went to work full-time on the farm. He really tried to do well but his heart wasn't in it, and restlessness was brewing inside him.

"I realized at age of 18 farming wasn't my cup of tea," he said.

After a steamy argument with Grandpa, Gilbert rolled up his extra pair of overalls and shirt and left for greener pastures. Rumor has it Grandpa was yelling "You'll never amount to anything" as Gilbert was packing to leave. Like I said before Grandpa just had to run things in the ground.

When Gilbert walked away from the familiar house and farm he weighed only 130 pounds but had a lot of determination to try something different. This turned out to be a life-changing decision, which led Gilbert to finding his own place in the sun. Sure enough, it wasn't in farming.

He went to stay with his sister Cleo and her husband Carlyle in nearby Lillington and started doing "public work." His first job was working at a saw mill and then later operating a fork lift. When Gilbert saw one of Cleo's neighbors, Isabelle Patterson, it was love at first sight, and the courting began. In March 1943 Gilbert received his draft notice and was scheduled for a physical examination. He and Isabelle were planning to marry after she graduated from high school but while riding to Dillon, S.C. with friends who were getting hitched, they decided to marry too, in case he was called to serve in World War II. As it turned out he was rejected due to a hernia and hearing loss.

The newlyweds rented two rooms in Sanford and Gilbert took a job at a food distributing company, earning $25 a week for 50 hours. He started off as a warehouse loader but did whatever was necessary — even if it meant sweeping the floor after he punched out to keep his job. Eventually he got into driving the delivery truck and selling some of their products.

He took a second job for extra income — after getting home from work he sold concessions during second shift at Edwards Motor Company, which manufactured airplane parts to supply armed forces during the war. Since he didn't have a car yet he walked to work, then back home, took a nap, and later pushed his food wagon through the plant again at midnight to accommodate the third shift workers. He sold sandwiches, soft drinks, candy and cigarettes — this was long before vending machines, mind you. This moonlighting venture added another $30 to his weekly pay.

The couple began to save a little money and soon bought a small four-room house with three ajoining lots for $1,300 in spring 1945. They were renting a room to two friends when the oil cooking stove exploded on a cold frosty morning in November 1945. Gilbert got the women out of bed, and all dashed to safety. By the time the fire department arrived the roof was falling in. "We lost everything we had," Gilbert said. With the $750 insurance settlement and a loan from his Mom and Dad, they soon rebuilt the house.

As war activities decreased, Edwards Company closed down and so did his concession stand. Gilbert took a job as route salesman for Pepsi-Cola, delivering 640 cases a week. He could have sold three times more but sugar rations curtailed production. Later he bought a distributorship for Swensen Foods and began selling the newest staples in the American diet — peanuts, potato chips, nabs, etc.

In 1947 Gilbert and Isabelle bought their first car, a 1937 Chevrolet for $130, and two years later purchased their   brand spanking new one — a 1949 sky blue Studebaker.

Finally his ambition and hard work paid off, and with two partners, he bought a kitchen cabinet/household fixture store that was going out of business in Sanford. Each put in $12,000 capital and owned one-third of Lee Cabinet and Store Fixture Company. Gilbert became manager, and with his captivating personality and award-winning smile he attracted customers. His business savvy caused sales to skyrocket, and soon he developed the company into Lee Builder Mart, which became the largest building supply company in a 50-mile radius.

Gilbert Lett stands in front of Lee Builder Mart in 1963

Gilbert had the Midas touch. He became involved in many other business ventures, including real estate development and stock investments. Things just seemed to turn to gold around him. Along the way he acquired 129 acres of our ancestors' original claim that includes Lett's Landing, from relatives, and has passed it on to his grandchildren. This is the seventh generation of Letts to own the land.

As Gilbert's bank account grew his sphere of influence increased — friends and family borrowed and often didn't pay back, but he loved them just the same. He has donated time and money to people and projects hither and yon. Building supplies have gone to many worthy causes. Cash has been given to numerous fund-raisers. Big checks to the local college have provided scholarships for deserving students.

In Broadway, near the school where he felt he wasn't up to par as a student, stands Lett Family Park, located on Gilbert Lett Road, so named because of his donation of nine acres. This park is an arena for ballgames and sports activities.

Gilbert's giving goes beyond lumber, land and money; for example, he has been known to take a friend to a widow's house and build her new steps. When a member of his extended family dies — which includes half of five counties — he rushes to pick up a barrel of chicken and head for the home and express his condolences. When the wake begins at the funeral home he's among the first to arrive and the last to leave. He makes sure he speaks to every member of the bereaved family and to everyone who knows everyone.

We joke in the family that Gilbert should have been a politician because he loves to talk to people and has attended more functions than anyone we know. But he's never had much patience for long business meetings or tolerance for boring board sessions where folks yakk all day. No, Gilbert is much too busy "doing" what other folks say they're going to do some day.

At 76, Gilbert doesn't miss a beat even though he's turned the building business over to his son Tony, daughter Janice and son-in-law Art, and nephew Steve. He has gone from 16-hour days to a more relaxing lifestyle. He's trying to work less and play more — fishing, dancing and traveling — and, of course, enjoying many activities with his three grandsons.

Through the years he's become accustomed to the finer things in life — big boats, new houses, fancy cars, fun cruises, and enjoyable trips to countries all over the world. His favorite toy is a 1991 Rolls Royce that he likes to share with newlyweds on their wedding day.

Every family has its shining star...one that burns more brightly than others, maybe at an early age when still wet behind the ears, sometimes as a young adult standing above those who settle for the settled-for life. Uncle Gilbert rose to greatness slowly and has taken his place in the sun to stay there forever. He's a source of pride and joy to his kinfolk, and we fondly call him "Mr. Rolls Royce."

People notice when Gilbert drives up in that Rolls Royce, not because he's a small man trying to look big in a fancy car but because he's a grand man in any car, in any house, in any setting, in every way. Gilbert is not just the generous patriarch of the Lett family, he's the king of caring in Lee County and beyond.

If Grandpa were alive today he's be yelling from the rooftop about his "mighty fine" son, and admitting that sure enough, "Shine" did amount to something big!

Chapter 23

Kissin' Cousins -- Colorful characters worth meeting

The good thing about my growing up with oodles of aunts and uncles is that there were also oodles of cousins -- and a vast sampling of different personalities. The diversity of relatives was almost as overwhelming as the variety of treats offered at Grandpa's country store.

In "Lettsville" I was surrounded by a cast of colorful characters who were kinfolk as well as the extended family who liked to stay a while at the old homeplace and "set a spell" at the country store.

While some folks just plain wore out their welcome, it was always nice that all I had to do when I wanted entertainment was to walk across the road. There was no end to the juicy gossip and dramatic tellings I could experience -- and everyone liked having me around because I gave up on ever trying to get a word in edgewise. I just let them yak to their heart's content and then wrote their stories in a diary, which I plan to sell someday to the highest bidder in the Buckhorn community or strike a deal with *The National Inquirer.*

My first close friendship with a cousin began with Lillian who lived the farthest away, in Virginia, and spent every summer with Gladys and Grandpa. She was the only person in the whole wide world who loved to play with paper dolls as much as I did.

Lillian and I also liked to dress up, and there were trunks of old clothes in the slanted storage areas behind the dormer windows. One day we happened upon some ole-timey frocks and decided to don them and pretend we were fancy ladies. Once we were sure we were irresistible we headed for the country store, expecting to amuse visitors and passersby.

Well, let me tell you when Grandpa spotted me, it was the first time I ever saw him speechless. He stared straight into my face and studied my dress carefully before finally stumbling out the words, "You look just like Miss Verta." I saw something shifting in Grandpa's face -- the hard jaw and fixed smile were replaced by a childlike softness as tears ran down his cheeks. Later I understood when Gladys said I was wearing one of Grandma's dresses. She also told me about a strange quirk about Grandma -- she said that when growing up Verta had blonde hair just like me, but that eventually it turned dark brown. She said the same thing happened to Gilbert -- his shiny blonde hair changed to black silk -- and she wondered if I was next in line.

She noted that I had "soot" black hair when born, and that was a sign that someday I'd probaby return to my "roots" hair color. (I'm still blonde and don't even have a gray hair in my head, let alone any dark ones, thank goodness!)

Back to cousins. Now let me tell you about Vernie Lett Womack, who owned a fabric store in Lillington in nearby Harnett County...or "Hornet," as we used to say. Her husband Lee built houses and developed real estate, and they were king and queen bees in the "Hornet" hive. Vernie was Ms. DAR (Daughters of the America Revolution) and Ms. Historian. She took it upon herself to take the time to research the Lett history long before anyone knew it was possible to search on the internet. She would often go to the archives and history building in Raleigh. One day she got so excited about finding information about our ancestors she forgot about time and when she came out her car was gone. Since Vernie grew up in Buckhorn community and had lived only in Lillington she had never heard of cars being stolen or towed. When she called the police (pronounced "poe-leece") to report the theft she discovered that her car had been empounded, and she had to pay to get it out.

Vernie loved every minute of her explorations.
She eventually published a book called *A History of
the Lett Family of the Upper Cape Fear River* with the
help of her fast typing niece, Barbara Cox. It turned out
"mighty fine" and sold like hot cakes.

Vernie was a soft-spoken, refined person and passed
on into the next world the same way she lived.
One Sunday after church, she ate at the homeplace,
attended a baby shower, went home, sat down in a chair,
and went gently into the night. After her death, her sister
Eula graciously became queen of genealogy, and at 80
she still remembers a lot of odds and ends about family
as well as other folks.

One time Eula told me a sweet story about her late
husband Gordon. She met him at a time when girls from
Broadway couldn't stand the boys from Boone Trail,
the high school in "Hornet" County. Initially she
resisted his flirting and wanted nothing to do with him
but got to know him better when they were riding
with some folks to work in Greensboro. Eula became
very sick with typhoid fever and was quarantined.

Gordon was working at a machine shop in Sanford and would go see her every night while others didn't dare go near her. Eventually she became "smitten" with him, and they got married in 1943. We were quite pleased 'cause Gordon became an expert at repairing televisions and fixed everyone's TV in Buckhorn and beyond.

Gordon is long gone, but Eula lives on, and she and Gilbert can tell you "pert-near" anything about the Lett family and even cousins twice removed, in fact, more than you want to know.

While growing up, our family of five spent every Christmas Eve with Uncle Gilbert and Aunt Isabelle, so I played with their children, Tony and Janice, more than the other cousins.

Jimmy, Tony, Carolyn, Janice, and "Sandy Lynn" Lett at Christmas 1959

Back in the late 1960s and early '70s, boy and girl relatives didn't hang out together much but Tony and I developed an unusual closeness. He liked to talk psychology and philosophy so we tended to converse about the meaning of life beyond Buckhorn, even past Sanford. Our friendship led to an arrangement for us to live together one year in college since his family had furnished him with a trailer, which they parked at Poverty Hill Trailer Park. When I told Dad I'd be staying with Tony, he said, "Have you lost your mind?" but he got used to the idea once he realized it was better to live with a male I knew than a strange roommate.

Like me Tony was breech born, which some folks used to say, was a sign of a peculiar child, and we tended to be oversensitive and more reflective of what was going on in our environment than other cousins. Janice's personality was totally different -- she was happy-go-lucky, and nothing bothered her.

Through the years I became closer to Tony and Janice because they were "citified" and liked the same things I did -- singing in church programs, attending drama productions, and dancing at fancy parties.

Both married the love of their life, Tony chose Rozie, and Janice spoke her vows with Art Coleman. While others in the family shook their heads and wondered what Tom, Dick or Harry I would date next, they opened their houses to these suitors, even the "ner-do-wells."

When I'd come home to visit I'd often stay with Janice and Art in their big two-story house where I had the privacy I valued while socializing with various kinfolks. Like me, Janice had to cope with some genetic weaknesses and health challenges, and as I explored unconventional approaches to healing, Janice noted my progress. Eventually I began treatment with a homeopath and healer Gene Dotson, started feeling and looking better than ever before, so Janice and Aunt Isabelle went to him too. While Uncle Gilbert teases us about going to that "root doctor" he is a little relieved that Janice and I don't have PMS anymore. However, he and others aren't impressed with the designer lettuce and herb tea I bring to family gatherings.

Family and friends pose in front of
Moore Union Congregational Christian Church

Tony and Janice have followed in the footsteps of their father and are now managing Lee Builder Mart, along with Art and a cousin Steve. I admire the way Janice and Tony and other relatives can live happily ever after with mates and thrive in chosen careers for a long time but somewhere along the way I realized that I had to follow the way of the writer and the call of the Muse.

Since coming back home I've discovered that I am very fortunate because I have two core families and several "branches" of the family tree who love me and welcome me into their homes. Writing my column, "Lett's Set a Spell," has opened up lines of communication with more kinfolk than ever before. Family members — even the ones who thought I was the most unusual — are beginning to think that "Sandy Lynn" just might have something to say, after all. So now, finally I'm no longer the black sheep of the family but a kissing cousin to all!

Chapter 24

Embracing Buckhorn and coming home to 'Sandy Lynn'

Throughout my life there is one thing that no one
has ever accused me of, and that is being normal,
so the idea of finding any sense of sanity became lost to
me for many years. The interesting thing about Life is
that it keeps us guessing, and just when we think
we have figured it out, it turns out not to be true.
Seems to me the more we know the less we know.

By the mid-1990s I had drawn upon a career in media — newspapers, magazines and television — in order to build my communications company. My business expanded from writing and editing to marketing and promotion and eventually emphasized professional speaking. Finally I had what I thought I wanted — lucrative clients and appreciative audiences — so why did I feel so restless and unfulfilled? I often addressed audiences about creating success but deep inside I felt like a failure. I continued to write numerous articles on health, but as I spoke to groups about renewing body, mind and spirit, I felt stressed and overwhelmed. Despite outer achievements my inner turmoil accelerated, and I could not make peace with my deep need for something more.

Yes, I had finally "made it big" but why didn't I feel "Most Likely to Succeed"?

When I promoted well-known authors I read their books and wondered why I had never pursued my own deepest dream of writing books. When I dared to write my truth I became enraptured in creativity, passionate and excited, lost in time and space. Ramblings of a free spirit do not pay the bills, my ego reminded me. Stories about my clients in publications did... ghost-written articles for my clients did.

"Why do I feel like a phony?," I asked my closest friends.

Who was this woman becoming known as a marketing guru and hanging out with the powerful people?

Where was the precious child who wrote poetry by the pond?

Who was this woman who wore my face and capitalized on my colorful personality?

Where was the darling girl who sang and danced on Mother Nature's stage?

Someone else was living my life and it wasn't me.

This other person was selling my intellect and ideas to clients — she was unscrupulously offering my talents and skills to the highest bidder.

Who was this woman who was moving my life in a direction I never wanted to go?

Somewhere along the way AlexSandra L. Lett, president of ALL Communications, had taken over Sandy Lynn's life. I had become an actress after all.

Several wake-up calls — an abusive relationship, a debilitating illness, an upsetting hurricane experience, and a frightening car accident — led me on a transformational journey into the depths of my soul.

I didn't feel comfortable sharing my trauma with my family but they sensed something was wrong because I rarely visited anymore. They encouraged me to move back to my home community, and we talked about my building a house at Lett's Landing or somewhere in Buckhorn community. Eventually I left behind my suburban home and materialistic lifestyle, and retreated to the country. In August 1998 I moved to a small cabin in the woods on the edge of a pond I named Paradise. I came to this picturesque setting looking for peace and purpose, seeking meaning and mission, asking for a miracle. I was determined to honor the deepest desire of my heart: to make peace with my past and to express myself as a writer.

My return to Sanford was met with mixed reviews. Some folks felt I had gotten "above my raisin'" or "too big for my britches." Many believed that when I went off to college — only 35 miles away but 35 years ahead of life on the farm — "Sandy" never came back. Even worse, I had realized, the creative and pioneering "Sandy Lynn" got lost somewhere along the way.

I can't remember the exact time I lost "Sandy Lynn," but I began to miss her. In striving to make it big in the World Out There I sacrificed the soulful little girl who wrote poetry by my family's pond. In searching for Life's Glamour I forgot the sweet child who loved the tall tales and the not-so-small people who told them. Each year these country folks get bigger and better...each day their stories more precious...each moment the memories closer to my heart.

I've learned to honor and admire the gifts Mom, Dad, Grandpa and Gladys and many others had to offer. I've come to understand that, like my Uncle Gilbert, I wasn't cut out for farming but need to respect the lessons learned from the farm — hard work, soft hearts, and steady faith always win out in the end.

Growing a business is a lot like sowing, tending and harvesting a crop. Creating, writing and publishing a book can be compared to giving birth to "young'uns" and raising them up right.

As I have come to draw upon the deep nourishment in my roots and get more in touch with the free spirit "Sandy Lynn" many blessings are coming my way. I have found my power as a person and am discovering a new voice as a writer. I enjoy writing my popular weekly column called "Lett's Set a Spell" about the salt-of-the-earth people connected to Buckhorn community, and my readers relish reading it. It doesn't take my audiences long to figure out what I have come to know, that life in Buckhorn is "mighty fine."

Grandpa's country store is still standing, filled with odds and ends from an era long gone but never to be forgotten. The walls hold the tall tales and juicy gossip that linger there.

Time passes but leaves a fragrance. I long to touch the essence of my ancestors, my family more intimately... to smell their sweet perfume...to recall a sacred way of life...to capture the stories for other generations.

I've published many articles about rich and famous people, health foods and big business, but nothing compares to the gentle souls I left behind, Mama's homemade dumplings, and the anchor business in Buckhorn community called Lett's Grocery and Filling Station.

Now that I'm back in Sanford, I often "set a spell" in the farmhouse where my parents have lived for more than half-a-century. These six rooms hold many emotions, more joy than sorrow. Recently I've seen Daddy wash my Mama's feet when she was sick. Only a few days ago I watched Mama gaze at Daddy with a bride's eyes. Someday I hope to look at someone that way. I admire that kind of old-timey commitment... "for better or for worse, for richer or for poorer, in sickness and in health."

Today I am honoring the richness of family bonds, enjoying the sense of community, and am relishing a closer connection with all the fine folks who once gathered in harmony at Grandpa's country store.

Now family and friends commune often at my parents' farmhouse where life is ripe for the pickin' every day.

Come on by and "set a spell"... the door's always open.

Home Sweet Home

"Sandy Lynn" with Mom and Dad in Buckhorn

Lett's Landing today

Lett's Set a Spell with

AlexSandra "Sandy Lynn" Lett

First and foremost AlexSandra "Sandy Lynn" Lett is a country girl who was raised near Lett's Landing, the site on the Cape Fear River where her ancestors from Ireland arrived 255 years ago. She is a native of Buckhorn community, located in the middle of Nowhere about 12 long miles from a Somewhere called Sanford and four miles from a no-stoplight town known as Broadway, "pert-near" 40 miles from Raleigh, the state capital of North Carolina.

The author — called "Sandy Lynn" when she didn't fit in to the mold of a traditional Southern farm girl — grew up writing, singing, and dramatizing. She "took a fancy" to the written word at an early age and was editor of her high school newspaper. When she attended college it was only 35 miles away but about 35 years ahead of her rural environment in terms of openness to new ideas and different lifestyles. She received a distinguished journalism scholarship at the University of North Carolina at Chapel Hill and graduated in 1976. Later she pursued graduate studies in communications at N.C. State University in Raleigh.

For several years AlexSandra wrote a weekly newspaper column called "Natural Living," which established her as an expert on preventative medicine and led to many speaking engagements. She published a book *Natural Living: From Stress to Rest* in 1984 and continues to endorse holistic approaches to healing body, mind and spirit.

In 1991 she founded ALL Communications in Raleigh, which offered writing, editing, marketing and public relations services. Soon afterwards she created TRANSFORMATIONS as the vehicle for offering programs on such topics as marketing, creating success, releasing stress, increasing energy, and enhancing communication.

In spring 2000 AlexSandra started writing a weekly column about colorful characters and saucy stories for a newspaper near Wilmington. The first installment, headlined "Set a Spell" at Grandpa's country store, was met with rave reviews from readers and led to numerous other articles. She is syndicating "Lett's Set a Spell" for distribution to various newspapers.

After the editor of a national publishing house applauded the merit of her columns and offered to publish a book in 2001 AlexSandra decided to do it herself. The result is *A Timeless Place, Lett's Set a Spell at the Country Store*. The publication of this book represents AlexSandra's awareness of how the creative, spontaneous and unique "Sandy Lynn" can be her authentic self and also live in harmony with the "mighty fine" folks from Buckhorn.

Through her company TRANSFORMATIONS AlexSandra continues to offer keynotes, seminars, workshops, and "funshops" on various topics, including bringing heart and soul to every area of our lives. Using a heavy Southern accent AlexSandra enjoys portraying "Sandy Lynn," who shares her views about the meaning of life with wit and wisdom.

For more information about speaking engagements and Southern dramatic performances by the author contact:

AlexSandra "Sandy Lynn" Lett
(919) 777-9362

 TRANSFORMATIONS

1996 Buckhorn Road
Sanford, NC 27330-9782, USA
LettsSetaSpell@aol.com

Visit the world wide web:
http://www.atimelessplace.com

Acknowledgements
to
"mighty fine" folks

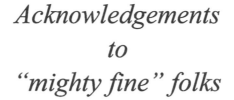

In the good old days women gathered together
to make a quilt, each doing what came naturally
and all contributing to the project in a special
way. Ideally life works that way. People join
forces to help each other, and they create
communities where each individual becomes
better when drawing upon the gifts of the group.
Writing this book reminded me of designing
a quilt, and without the support of many others
I could not have created this masterpiece of
many colors.

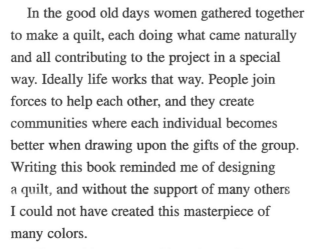

When writing my weekly column, "Lett's
Set a Spell," and other projects, I asked others
to   look at my works of art, which could be
compared to carefully crafted quilt squares.
Many "mighty fine" folks have given me constant
feedback and encouragement about my writing.

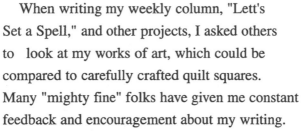

Those who have contributed most to my finding a new voice as a Southern writer are David Clegg, Tracey Daley, Deborah Batts, Joanna Bright, Jane Norton, Donna Dutton, Lynn Garren Henderson, Kay Gilley, Jackie Parker, Jinger Gibson, Susan Beal, Lois Thomas, Ellen Ferguson, Diana Henderson, Judy Fourie, Betsy Dupree, Candace Gale, Saphriel Anderson, Valerie Kelly, Marj Marie, Joan Rose, J.B. Shelton, Cathy Kielar, Deb Mangis, and Gene and Maria Mele Dotson.

I want to express appreciation to some key individuals:

Renay Wulpern of Jones Printing Company, who coordinated the graphics and photos for *A Timeless Place* and who exquisitely created various quilt squares for each chapter;

Diane and Rick LaFata, who recognized "a good hair day" and took a snapshot that ended up on the back cover;

Erin Fredrich, an editor at Andrews McMeel Publishing, who complimented my prose and poetry, described me as an "awesome" writer, and who continues to encourage me;

Christine Testolini, a marketing consultant and a former agent, who advised me on my various writing projects and suggested I discover my voice as "a powerful Southern woman";

Deborah Batts, my Chief Financial Officer, who is helping me take my talent and products into the marketplace;

Jim McBride, president of Affiliated Warehouse Companies, Inc., who ordered 250 copies of this book as Christmas presents for friends and clients;

leaders and participants in the Legacy Center of Chapel Hill, especially NC32, who urged me to reinvent myself so I could stand for transformation in myself and others;

participants in Spirit & Business, who helped me understand that work is spelled Work, and relates to purpose, passion, creativity and excellence;

Herbert Lett, publisher of the *Carolina Beach/Kure Beach Weekly News,* who asked me to write a weekly column originally called "Lett It All Hang Out";

Jay Twaite, editor of *The Sanford Herald,* the first newspaper to buy my "Lett's Set a Spell" column;

numerous readers, family members and friends, who have told me and/or sent e-mails to say that my writings make them laugh, cry, and sometimes get cold chills, and that my intended words of wit and wisdom touched their lives:

the many patrons who have realized free spirits focused on their creativity welcome monetary contributions;

and generous givers galore, including: Caroline Thomas, Joani Merritt, Shellie Merritt, Judy Hamberg, J.P. Poisson, Alex Candelaria, Sally Parker, Bill Horner Jr., Bob Angell, Nancy Callihan, Bil and Cher Holton, Jack and Marsha Graf, Beth and Bernie Ashman, Drew Becker, George Ward, Ann and Cy Klosterman, Diana Hales, Lori Binder, Barbara Hemphill, Darleen Johns, Carolyn Grant, Sheila Hale Ogle, Lana Calloway Zenner, Nona Manchester, Kim Wise, Kathy Aalfs, Christine DeLorey, George Smart, Rick King, Joe Bauerband, Joe Bauerband Jr., Steve and Melissa Nystrom, and of course, all my Legacy and Unity Church connections.

My column and this book have opened lines of communication with my family that will continue to develop. I am especially grateful for historical information and/or pictures from Gilbert Lett, Eula Wilson, Nathan and Mary Alice Crissman, Diane Lett Thomas, Maxine Thomas Patterson, Lillian Crabtree, and the late Vernie Womack, author of *A History of the Lett Family of the Upper Cape Fear River.*

While some of my closest kinfolks are not mentioned in the book, I appreciate everyone in my family. Each has touched my writing, my life and my heart in many ways.

I want to acknowledge my core family, my father and mother, Puzie Doyle (Bud) and Ruby Knight Lett, my sister Carol McNeill and her husband Pete; my brother Jimmy and his wife Sharon; my nephews Wayne, Billy, Todd and their wives Emily, Kim, and Tracey, respectively, and Mark. I must mention my most valuable treasures: my great-nieces Chelsey and Tyler, and my great-nephews Jared, Joshua and Jacob. We get together often to "set a spell" at Mom and Dad's farmhouse, the most sacred space we have ever known.

I appreciate my second family -- Gilbert and Isabelle Lett, my cousin Janice Lett Coleman and her husband Art; and my cousin Tony and his wife Rozie, and their three sons, Jonathan, Nicholas, and Matthew Lett.

I thank God that I am so blessed with family and friends who support my journey on this planet is so many different ways and am eternally grateful for God's role in my life.

This book is like a quilt that should be equally precious to both the giver and the receiver -- my intention is that people will share it with folks they love the most. It is a rare work of art because many hands and many hearts came together to create it. I believe that everybody we meet is a thread in Life's tapestry and that every experience is a fiber in Life's fabric. Each thread, each fiber brings color and texture that touches the core of our beingness. Every person and everything in our lives are blessings if we allow them to bring us closer to our authentic selves and to enhance our never-ending transformation!

A Timeless Place
Lett's Set a Spell at the Country Store

ORDER FORM

$19.95 x   number of books   _____

Postage/handling* (see below)   _____

TOTAL PRICE   _____

*Postage in the United States
$4 for one book, $6 for two books, $7 for three books,
$8 for four books, $9 for five books, $10 for six to nine books

*Postage outside the United States
$10 for one book, $12 for two books, $13 for three books,
$14 for four books, $15 for five books, $16 for six to nine books

Free book and free postage with every order of 10 books

6% sales tax per $1 for North Carolina residents

Name _____

Address _____

Phone Numbers _____

E-mail Address_____

Credit Card Number_____Expiration Date _____

Names to be used for autographed copies _____

Send orders with checks or money orders to

TRANSFORMATIONS
1996 Buckhorn Road
Sanford, NC 27330-9782, USA

To place orders call: (919) 777-9362